UNDERSTANDING the HUMAN VOLCANO

"*Understanding the Human Volcano* should be required reading for every student. Educators, parents, law enforcers, and youth-serving professionals can benefit equally from Hipp's succinct and articulate insights."

— Ronald D. Stephens, Ed.D.
Executive director, National School Safety Center

▼ ▼ ▼

"Long overdue, Hipp's book for teens is the most comprehensive and reader-friendly guide on violence prevention I have read. He covers the main points in a thoughtful, nonshaming manner."

— Mary Atwater
Violence prevention coordinator
Jefferson County (Colorado) Public Schools

▼ ▼ ▼

"Teens and their parents will *want to read* Mr. Hipp's book. He presents real-life solutions that empower youth to break violent cycles, such as bullying."

— Mary Grace Reed
Member, Farmington (Connecticut) Board of Education
and the Capitol Region Education Council

▼ ▼ ▼

"In this book, young people candidly voice their deepest concerns about violence. Earl Hipp offers them viable solutions to reduce violence in its varied forms."

— Patricia McPhearson Davis
Safe and Drug-Free Schools and Communities manager
Chicago Public Schools

UNDERSTANDING the HUMAN VOLCANO

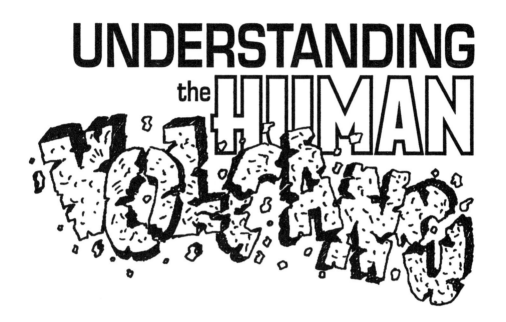

What Teens Can Do about Violence

by Earl Hipp

illustrations by L. K. Hanson

HAZELDEN®

INFORMATION & EDUCATIONAL SERVICES

Hazelden
Center City, Minnesota 55012-0176

1-800-328-0094
1-651-213-4590 (Fax)
www.hazelden.org

ISBN: 1-56838-359-2

Editor's note

The list of behaviors and conditions that are common to people with
the potential to harm themselves or others, printed on pages 49–50,
is reprinted with permission. It was developed by the National School
Safety Center; ©1998; Dr. Ronald D. Stephens, Executive Director;
141 Duesenberg Drive, Suite 11, Westlake Village, California 91362;
phone (805) 373-9977; fax (805) 373-9277; www.nssc1.org.

04 03 02 01 00 6 5 4 3 2 1

Cover illustrations and interior illustrations by L. K. Hanson
Cover design by Terri Kinne
Interior design and typesetting by Spaulding & Kinne

Contents

PART 1

The Problem of Violence in Our World

Contents 〜〜〜〜〜〜〜〜〜〜〜〜〜〜〜〜〜〜

Acknowledgments

Thanks to you for being interested in reducing violence and for caring enough to want to learn more.

Thanks to all the young people who took the time to send me their heartfelt and sometimes painful stories, thoughts, and even poems. They did so because they wanted to do their part to reduce violence in the world. Their honesty, courage, and commitment bring life and energy to the book.

Thanks to the many thousands of adults working with young people in families, schools, and communities. In sometimes unbelievably difficult conditions, these people do their very best to create safe and nurturing environments so kids can develop their full potential. A huge THANK-YOU to parents, teachers, administrators, counselors, social workers, school volunteers, people in law enforcement, those in spiritual communities, and the many others who want the world to be wonderful for young people. You are my sheroes and heroes and deserve all the thanks, praise, and recognition I can offer.

Thanks to all the people who helped the book come to life: All the supportive people who put me in touch with kids, including Ann DeHoff, Linda Tucker, Mary Hoopman, Sally Dale, and Clara Buckanaga; my totally amazing Web master, Matt Cohen; my ferociously competent contract attorney, Debra Kass Orenstein; the Reed editorial team, including Mary Grace, Eric, Keith, and Craig; the leadership and contributors at Red Wing correctional facility and Boys' Totem Town, and the caring circle of my very supportive Friends from the 1900 meeting.

Special thanks to a few others:

To Gwen, my unbelievably patient and supportive partner in life. All my love and thanks for being you and encouraging me to be me.

Thanks to my partner on this book, artist L. K. Hanson. He makes this difficult subject more understandable through his incredible graphic talents. I am blessed in our friendship. My life and the world are much improved because he's around.

Thanks to all the editors and other talented staff at Hazelden who are so good and care so much about making a difference. But a special and very large THANKS to my editor, Cynthia Harris. Writing is really rewriting and rewriting. In the process of creating a book about this large and difficult subject, I found her support, editorial skills, and keen objectivity invaluable. If you ever decide to write a book, pray for an editor like Cynthia.

Finally, I want to honor and express my gratitude to the spiritual force in my life that is making it all possible. I'm humbled and blessed to be used in this way.

About the Author

Earl Hipp is a writer and speaker who lives in Minneapolis, Minnesota, in the summer and in Tucson, Arizona, in the winter. He likes to spend time with his friends and family, hike in the mountains, fly airplanes, rollerblade, and use the Internet.

He wants to get letters or e-mail from readers. You can visit this book's Web site and leave an e-mail message, or you can write Earl to tell him your stories, share your experiences with human volcanoes, discuss violence prevention, offer your ideas for another book, or just say hi.

Earl can be reached at:
Human Resource Development, Inc.
2938 Monterey Avenue
Minneapolis, MN 55416

E-mail: Ehipp@TheHumanVolcano.com
Web site: *http://www.thehumanvolcano.com*
   Or:
Earl Hipp, Author
Hazelden Information and Educational Services
P.O. Box 176
Center City, MN 55012-0176

About the Illustrator

L. K. Hanson, in addition to being an illustrator and cartoonist for the Minneapolis *Star Tribune,* has illustrated many books for Hazelden. He lives in Minneapolis, Minnesota.

About the Kids Who Contributed to This Book

The personal stories and quotes in this book arrived by mail, fax machine, and computer. Some kids picked pen names to protect their identity. Contributions came from all over the world, and we included the locations of those farthest away. We also chose to let readers know when a contributor wrote from a correctional facility.

Introduction

It's funny how the inspiration for a book comes to find you. The book in your hands is a result of a series of events that happened pretty close together. These experiences helped me to find the nerve to write a book on the huge topic of violence prevention and to dedicate it to some special people.

The first inspiration was a letter I received from a 17-year-old man in prison. I like hearing from my readers and get a lot of mail, but this one stood out. It began with the plea: "Mr. Hipp, you have to help me with my anger...." This smart but lonely young man had a tendency toward rage and violence that had landed him in prison and was getting him into more trouble as he struggled to deal with the pressures of prison life. He was reaching out for help to cope with the angry and explosive part of himself. I wrote back to support him in his struggle. Since then, I've received many more painful letters from other young men who were incarcerated.

So the first dedication of this book is for the many thousands of young people who learned violence as a way of life in their families, schools, or communities and who now find themselves in some form of prison as a result. This book and my heart go out to you.

Then came the shooting at Columbine High School in Littleton, Colorado. Two smart but lost and very confused boys, fueled by anger, used their creativity in tragic ways. As the world reeled in the "whys" of grief, I joined those who wanted to understand what happened and to do something to help. In my research, I came upon a Web site created to send messages of healing to the Columbine community. A young man who used the name Timothy wrote a message that inspired my hope that people can change. He wrote a sad tale of growing up with "people putting me down, mocking me, ostracizing me." He wrote about how that led him to become part of a small but very dangerous group of young people who tried to blow up their school's winter ball and had planned to "execute a massacre just like the one in Columbine." A spiritual awakening led him to change however. He writes: "I turned away from the gang and it generally disbanded. When I heard of Littleton, I found out that my dreams turned nightmares had come true.... I know what it's like to be a member of a gang like the trenchcoat mafia.... It's only through the change of our views that we can truly see how to prevent these things."

The second dedication of the book is for all those young people who live with the hurt, deep rage, and isolation that drives these desperate acts. I hope that in this book they will find a hand of caring and support they can use to climb out of their pain. Everyone who helped bring this book to life did so because they want to help young people in this kind of pain. So this book and especially my heart go out to any potential human volcanoes, bubbling inside with rage and despair, ready to erupt.

Another event that motivated me to write this book occurred when a group of kids beat up a young friend of mine at school. I was reminded of my own nightmarish childhood experiences with bullying. I rediscovered the old anger that *still* lives in me as a result.

The third dedication of the book is for anyone who is a target of bullying, but also for the people who do the bullying. It is my hope that in this book you will find some help and understanding. This book and my heart go out to you.

The final inspiration came as I seriously began to consider writing the book. I started to pay attention to the violence around me. I realized that in so many ways and so very rapidly the world was becoming more violent and frightening. Violent eruptions by human volcanoes, although extremely scary, are actually infrequent. The vast majority of the violence that touches our lives comes from a combination of many other influences: the little acts of violence all of us do to those around us; the violence that results from our conscious or unconscious intolerance of people who are different from us; the everyday violence that happens in families, schools, and communities; and the violence that constantly assaults us through television programming, news, music, movies, and even computers. This bubbling core of violence influences all of our lives.

The scary thing is that as these forms of violence grow, our denial grows too. We become desensitized to all but the most obscene acts. Because there is so much violence around us, we often feel powerless. We may be tempted to believe we cannot make a positive difference. But when people take this position, violence has fertile ground in which to continue to grow in the world and in our lives.

So the final dedication is to anyone reading this book. You probably wouldn't be reading this unless you want to do something about violence. Unless each of us becomes willing to take action, the violence in the world around us *will* get worse. So I dedicate this book to you in the hope that it will inspire you to do the things you can to reduce violence. This book and my heart go out to you.

Let's go make a difference!

Part 1

The Problem of Violence in Our World

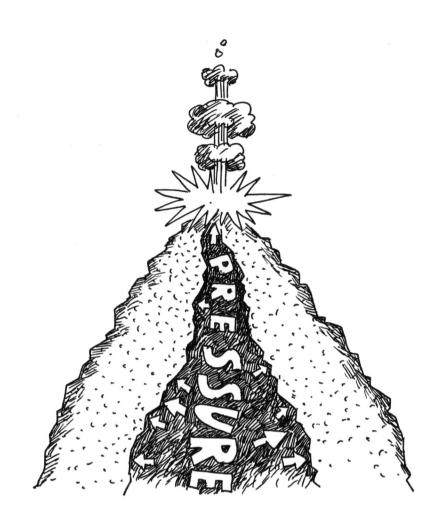

 **CHAPTER 1**

The Bubbling Core of Violence

Deep inside a volcano is a core of hot magma. As it bubbles away, the internal pressures from the gases it releases gradually build. Most of the time volcanoes cook away with almost no visible sign of their amazing power and potential for disaster. But when a volcano can no longer contain the powerful internal forces, it erupts violently.

The explosion can be so intense that it blows off the whole mountaintop, sending out molten lava, fiery rocks, and smothering ashes that destroy everything for miles around.

Before an eruption, people who live close to a volcano can be unaware of what's going on because they're not paying attention to the signals the volcano gives off. Or they may be aware that the volcano is cooking away but not admit to themselves how severe the consequences of a major eruption would be. When the big explosion happens, however, everyone close to the volcano feels the impact of the destructive forces. Sometimes the fallout can be traced around the globe.

In much the same way, violence bubbles away in the world around us. We're all exposed to a variety of influences that teach us about and even encourage violence in our daily lives. Yet like those who live near a volcano, we sometimes seem unable or unwilling to recognize the growing danger of our situation—until a human volcano explodes.

Very much like a real volcano, the most extreme human volcanoes erupt with unimaginable violence that kills people and permanently alters the lives of survivors. In communities where someone sets off a bomb or takes a gun into a school, place of worship, or workplace, people experience physical and emotional trauma that is almost impossible to comprehend. Life for those up close to the explosion is changed forever.

With the instantaneous visual communication made possible by television and the Internet, the rest of us become virtual eyewitnesses to these seemingly

> **"Sometimes things happen so fast, you get to a point of uncontrolled anger and you just snap."**
> — Simone, 16

> **"It is very scary like the shootings in Littleton, Colorado. Even though I live a long way away, at first I was scared to go back to school."**
> — Kate, 11

random acts of violence. Even though most of us will never experience tragedies of these proportions directly, our sense of safety and security may be shattered by them. We are all touched by the suffering of the people in the path of a human volcano, and we all feel a little more scared and vulnerable.

Although human volcanoes may appear to erupt out of the blue, they have usually been bubbling away for a while. The pressures that have built up inside are the result of a powerful mix of life-shaping forces. To better understand why human volcanoes erupt, we need to learn a little about canaries.

The Miner's Canary

Coal mines often contain life-threatening gases that can't be seen or smelled. Today high-tech equipment carefully monitors the safety of the air in mines. But before this equipment existed, coal miners would take along a canary for insurance. Because canaries are small and fragile, they are extremely sensitive to dangerous gases. A canary's death in the mine provided an early warning system that something was very wrong. When the bird died, the miners knew they'd be in trouble soon and went running for their lives.

Just like the gases in the old mines, the violence in the world around us is very dangerous and hard to monitor. The human volcanoes who explode with terrible acts of violence are very much like the fragile canaries. For many reasons, human volcanoes are uniquely vulnerable to the toxic influences in our violent world. They warn us that something is terribly wrong in our social environment and that we should all be scrambling to do something about it.

Every day we all absorb messages that promote violence. We gradually increase our tolerance and become comfortable with higher and higher levels of violence. As these influences work on each of us, we become a little more likely to be violent in our relationships, a little more likely to become a victim or to witness a violent act.

But instead of doing something to reduce the violence, we allow violent messages to flood into our lives through movies, song lyrics, television, sports, and computer and video games. We zone out during news reports of violent gang activity and the people killed with easily obtained guns. We filter out countless expressions of frustration, anger, or even hate that occur in our families, neighborhoods, schools, and communities. We all know of people who have been yelled at, made fun of, insulted, discriminated against, blackmailed, hit, pushed around, threatened, or even stabbed or shot. But unless something happens to us or to the people we care about, or unless an incident is violent enough to shock us, we often ignore it. We think of violence as someone else's problem. We believe there's nothing we can do.

> "I live in a small town of six thousand people. The town was quiet until a few years back when small gangs started popping up and teenagers started packing knives and guns. I used to feel safe here, but now I don't."
>
> — Maggie, 17

All of these violent acts and messages melt into a hot, bubbling core of violence that simmers beneath the surface of our lives. Like miners who didn't pay attention to the canary, if we ignore the warning signs from human volcanoes, we'll all be at high risk from the toxic influences that surround us. To learn what we can do about this problem, we have to learn about elephants.

The Whole Elephant

According to an old story, one day an elephant wandered into a village where people had no eyes. As you can imagine, this unusual event caused a commotion, and soon a small crowd gathered around to try to understand this amazing creature. Being a friendly elephant, it let the villagers move in close and touch it. A man who felt a leg said, "This creature must be tall and strong, for where it touches the ground it's very sturdy and round." A woman who grasped the elephant's ear replied, "No, I think it can fly rapidly because of its large, thick wings." Another man who held just the elephant's trunk said, "I don't think it flies at all. It's flexible like a snake, so it obviously moves along the ground."

On and on the discussion went, with each villager expressing a different opinion about the unusual creature. But no one had the whole picture. No one understood the whole elephant or its true power and form.

In much the same way, many people who talk about the problem of violence tend to focus on just one issue. According to these people,

the real problem is all about . . . the divorce rate, or the lack of moral values, or single-parent families, or poor parenting skills, or drugs, or weak punishment for juvenile offenders, or youth alienation and isolation, or poverty, or the lack of emotional development in young boys, or the absence of violence prevention programs, or violent music lyrics, or shoot-em-up TV shows, or point-and-shoot computer games, or the easy availability of guns and other weapons, or a shortage of school counselors and other helping professionals . . . and on and on and on.

In fact, each of those issues contributes to the problem of violence in our world. But if we focus on just one of them, we're like the sightless villagers who can't grasp the whole elephant. We have to stand back to see the amazing complexity of this huge problem.

It's hard to imagine the number of people and incredible amount of activity it will take to get the violence in our society under control. Given the sheer size of the challenge, it's easy to give in to feelings of hopelessness and inaction. But then a human volcano explodes somewhere, shattering our illusion of safety, and reminds us that we each must act.

In part 2 of this book we'll explore a number of things you can do to help reduce violence in our world. But before we begin, we have to understand this powerful force called violence and why some people become human volcanoes.

> **"Ten years ago, if we saw someone being mugged on television, we would have been shocked and stunned. Now it takes a bloody murder . . . to even get a reaction. If we do not react to television, will we react to someone being attacked in our community?"**
>
> — Kate, 16, New Zealand

Words

Looks

Signs

Acts

What Is Violence?

When we think of violence, we often think of the big stuff: war, terrorism, gangs, shootings, or the explosion of a human volcano that leaves a community full of victims. This is the violence that makes newspaper headlines or the evening news. We hear about the big stuff all the time, and although it usually doesn't involve us or those we know, it's out there and it's scary.

But what is even scarier is that the worst acts are just a small part of all the violence around us. It's the millions of small acts that happen every day that make all of us victims and perpetrators (people who commit violence). If you're willing to take a close look, you'll discover that we all either experience or engage in some form of violence every day. While some people are much more violent than others, we are all a little guilty.

Because violence is complicated and takes so many forms, it's hard to have a simple definition. *Respect & Protect*, a great curriculum about a process for reducing school violence, says that violence is committed when someone uses "any mean word, look, sign, or act that hurts a person's body, feelings, or things." That not only covers school shootings but also includes those times when you're angry and yell at someone.

Although acts of physical violence are obvious, emotional violence sneaks into many parts of our lives. Disrespectful, degrading, demeaning, or intimidating words, looks, and signs can wound our feelings. And don't forget the hurtful effects of social violence, subtle acts like not listening when someone is talking to you, letting someone down by not showing up when you said you would, isolating people you don't like by not letting them in your group, or just being mean in one of a million other ways. Given this definition of violence, it can be easy to understand how each of us contributes to the problem.

"One day a friend of mine stood me up over a movie. I was so furious. The next day when I saw her, I just went off. Without thinking, I called her every name in the book and then we got into a fistfight. When the smoke cleared, I burst into tears and began apologizing for my behavior. Not meaning to, I had hurt my best friend verbally and physically."

— Maggie, 17

Here is a short list of some of the many ways violence shows up in our behavior:

○ *Words*—putting down someone, mean teasing, using negative nicknames or racial slurs, making threats, criticizing constantly, insulting people or their relatives, ordering someone around, using sexual language or swearing, writing names in restrooms, passing intimidating notes, telling lies, starting rumors.

Words

▶ **"I had this thick coat to keep me warm in the cold**
▶ **Minnesota winter. Well, this guy John thought it**
▶ **would be funny to call me names like 'Whale.' He**
▶ **would tease me endlessly and almost pushed me**
▶ **to suicide with all the name-calling he did."**
▶ — Nicky, 14

○ *Signs*—aggressive hand gestures, like giving someone the finger, making a fist, or drawing a finger across the throat; sexual gestures, like mooning or crotch-grabbing; gang symbols, a threatening tattoo, clothing meant to offend or intimidate.

▶ "One time in first grade, I saw these fourth-graders

▶ flicking off another boy on our bus. I thought it was

▶ a cool thing because a bunch of others were laugh-

▶ ing about it. Thinking this, I played follow-the-leader

▶ and flicked the boy off too. At the time I had no

▶ idea what I was doing. The boy became a social

▶ outcast in the years to come. As I remember doing

▶ that, I feel like I have contributed to his misery."

▶ — Spoe, 14

○ *Looks*—staring aggressively, making mean faces, leering, using threatening body postures, rolling your eyes to indicate disgust.

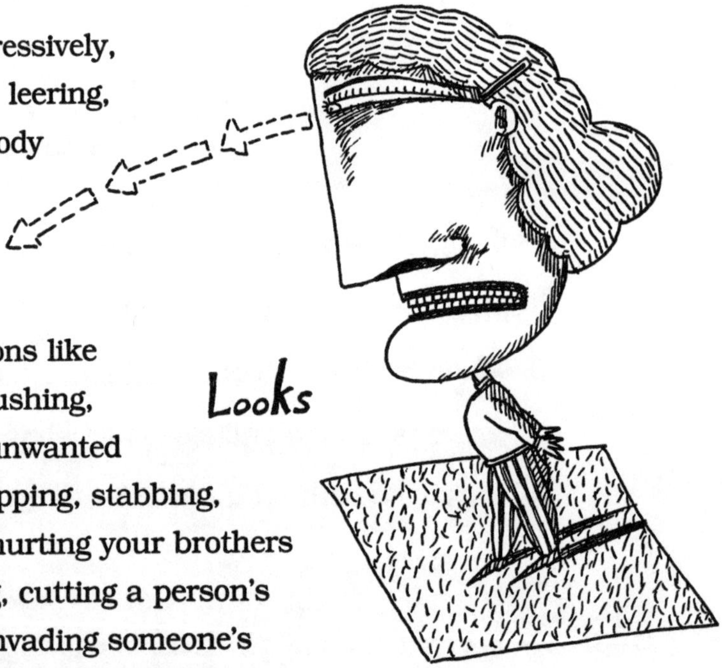

Looks

○ *Acts*—physical actions like hitting, pinching, pushing, kicking, grabbing, unwanted sexual touching, tripping, stabbing, shooting, stealing, hurting your brothers and sisters, spitting, cutting a person's hair, purposefully invading someone's personal space, spray-painting someone's things, dumping books, displaying a weapon, scratching the paint on a car or bike, tearing someone's clothes, using an aggressive pet to intimidate someone.

What all violent words, signs, looks, and acts have in common is that they inflict physical pain, hurt feelings, damage property, or instill fear. Violence, no matter how small an act or how seemingly innocent the intention, means the victim suffers some degree of hurt or pain. While some acts are way more hurtful than others, all violence leaves some type of wound or emotional scar.

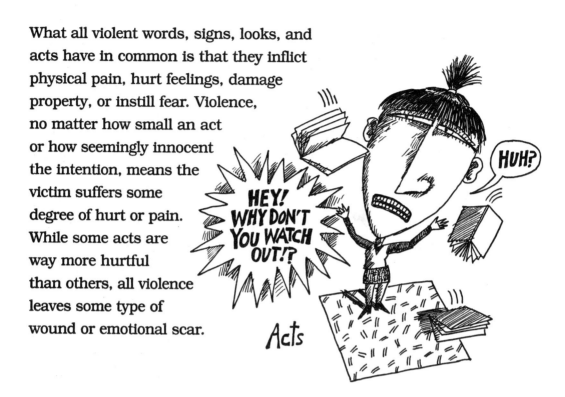

▶ **"In eighth grade I was in the Drama Club. There was**
▶
▶ **a girl there who was kinda rude, and she made me**
▶
▶ **mad. Halfway through the class we were on the**
▶
▶ **stage practicing for our play, and I tripped her and**
▶
▶ **made her fall off the stage. I got sent home early**
▶
▶ **and was taken out of the play."**
▶
▶   — April, 15

The Continuum of Violence

It may be helpful to think of violence as causing a range of hurt and pain that goes from what you might consider "no big deal" up to serious physical or emotional injury. Clearly, teasing your little brother on a rare occasion does not cause as much pain as an all-out fistfight with someone you don't like, which is not as bad as shooting someone. Some acts are just worse than others.

But from the outside, you can't always tell how much pain someone feels on the inside. That's why an important way to measure the seriousness of a violent act is to try to look at it from the perspective of the person on the receiving end. How intense is the physical or emotional pain he or she feels?

> ▶ **"Violence can affect**
> ▶
> ▶ **people more than**
> ▶
> ▶ **you ever know.**
> ▶
> ▶ **Whatever kind of**
> ▶
> ▶ **violence it is, it's**
> ▶
> ▶ **never good."**
> ▶
> ▶ — Maria, 16

We each have a different tolerance for violence. What might be devastating for one person may be no big deal for another. And to make things even more complex, the effects of a lot of small acts of violence can add up. For a person who has been bullied month after month, the last straw could be just being pushed into a locker. This one act could ignite a huge and violent explosion.

With these measures of hurt and pain in mind, we can develop a list of violent behaviors that go from the smaller acts up to those that cause enormous pain. Because each of us is unique, we all have different opinions about which forms of violence are the worst. If you were making the list, you might arrange things differently. But the following list gives us a way to start thinking about how some acts are worse than others. This list is adapted from the continuum of violence in *Respect & Protect:*

o no violence

o rolling eyes or laughing at someone

o starting rumors/gossiping

o giving the finger or using other aggressive gestures

o mean teasing/put-downs

o destructive self-talk

○ name-calling or verbal taunting

○ being "in" and excluding others

○ graffiti/vandalism

○ damaging someone's things

○ hurting animals

○ stealing

○ sexual harassment through language or gestures

○ angry yelling

○ spitting, bumping, shoving, tripping, or blocking

○ intimidation, blackmail, or threats

○ punching, kicking, or slapping

○ reckless driving or driving under the influence of alcohol or other drugs

○ self-violence like bulimia, anorexia, or intentionally cutting yourself

○ threatening with a weapon

○ attempting suicide

○ sexual assault

○ shooting or stabbing someone

○ suicide/homicide

○ killing lots of people

On this list of violent acts, can you draw a line where above the line you'd have "acceptable violent behavior" and below "unacceptable violent behavior"? Where would you draw that line on the violence continuum?

Can you

think of

a form

of violent

behavior

that is

okay?

No form of violent behavior is okay. Some are justified but not okay.

- Brooklynn, 17

Hitting a pillow or a punching bag to let out those feelings and urges, not a person.

- Janine, 17

Maybe spanking a young child, but as long as it's not hard and it's just to teach them a lesson. But that's pretty borderline because it's hard to draw the line between spanking and violence.

- Brianna, 13

Self-defense, when you're being attacked.

- Sarita, 16

Yes, when you are in war and you are fighting for your country.

- JD, 13

Some people think that verbal violence is acceptable, but I don't think it's okay.

- Maria, 16

Sports, football, etc.

- Lukkas, 16

I don't think there is an okay form of it; violence is violence. Someone always ends up getting hurt, whether it's physically or emotionally.

- Nicole, 16

Where to Draw the Line

Tolerance of violent behavior varies greatly from person to person, family to family, school to school, and community to community. In each case, the rules about what is "acceptable" violent behavior and what crosses the line into "unacceptable" violent behavior are very different. But if we are going to reduce the violence in our lives, we have to think about where we, as individuals, are going to draw that line. Can you think of a form of violence that is really okay with you? That means that you can accept the hurt and pain the victim feels as a result.

Ideally, the best place to draw the line is at "No violence." That means *no* amount of hurt and pain *any* victim would feel is acceptable. But we don't live in a perfect world with perfect people. We live in a world full of violent influences, and we all have our moments, those times when our own behavior is violent in small or sometimes big ways.

> ▶ **"Violence will never**
> ▶ **solve your problems.**
> ▶ **No matter how bad**
> ▶ **you feel, reacting**
> ▶ **violently will only**
> ▶ **make it worse."**
> ▶ — Casey, 17

That's why after the line at "No violence," the next most critical stopping point is the *instant* after any form of violence occurs. When we experience or witness a behavior we feel is violent, we must name it as unacceptable and if at all possible, do something about it.

Why We Must Draw the Line

While there are thousands of reasons to take a stand against violence, here are three important ones for you to think about.

Say No or Say Go

Pretending that violence isn't happening is *the same thing* as saying it's all right to be violent. If people in families, schools, and communities don't take a strong stand, it's like saying, "It's not worth the effort

> **"Violence is never the answer. If you hurt someone badly, you also hurt their family and friends. So it starts a chain reaction of anger. So stop the chain before it starts."**
>
> — Brooklynn, 17

to step in. We'll put up with violence until something *so* bad happens, we have to act." That's why anything short of a loud and visible NO is a GO to violence.

Violence thrives when we pretend not to notice it, are silent, and take no action. Where people are okay with a "little" violence around them, it becomes rooted and grows. You can be sure that in such an environment, violent behavior will be repeated and get worse. The only options are to put up with increasing levels of violence in our lives or draw the line that says violence must stop here and now.

Violence Makes Things Worse

Violence means there are victims, people who suffer hurt and pain. Even when violence seems to be justified—to protect your family or to stop a crime—people get injured, witnesses are terrified, someone gets angry, and thoughts of revenge show up. Violence sometimes defuses a really bad situation, but there is still always someone worse for the experience.

Not only does violence make things worse, but the more violent the behavior, the stronger the negative impact it has. The larger the rock you throw in a pond, the bigger the waves that roll out across the surface. In the same way, yelling at your brother may upset only you, him, and the dog. But if someone comes into your school and starts shooting, the act changes lives of people near and far, forever. The more intense the violence, the greater the damage. Whenever people engage in violence, things get worse—sometimes a lot worse.

Violence Moves in Circles

When people experience violence, they always have feelings—often big feelings. If they hurt enough, they may want revenge. If they act on that feeling, the whole circle starts again and may continue endlessly.

In the news, we hear about wars that are the most recent round in a circle of violence dating back hundreds of years. Closer to home, the same thing happens in rival gangs, between family members, and among people who've been mean to one another. Every time someone reacts to violence with violence, the whole circle starts again.

If you understand how this circle works and don't want to pay the price for being involved, you can end the cycle by drawing a line. You can learn to say, "I'm not going to respond to violence with violence. The circle of violence stops with me." (See "End the Circle of Violence," pages 82–85.)

> "What goes around comes around."
>
> — Licia, 13

> "I kicked a friend of my little brother off of my property with force. The next day he and his friends beat me up, and I realized violence really is a cycle."
>
> — Johnny, 16

 CHAPTER 3

The Lessons of Violence

Because there is so much violence around us, we often take it for granted. It's kind of like all the stuff lying around in your room that you don't notice until a guest says something or you go away for a few days and return to see it with fresh eyes. In a way, even though things are in plain sight, they're hidden from your view. The technical term for this is *desensitized*.

Being desensitized to violence means we don't see it around us, or if we do, we don't have the feelings or sensations we should feel when we witness it.

If you see someone being shot on TV, it's probably not scary. If you blow apart a character in a computer game, you probably don't feel bad. If you see a little kid in your neighborhood playing with a toy gun, you probably don't feel frightened. It means that some forms of violence have become "normal" because we've gotten used to them. After a while we get so comfortable with low levels of violence that only the more intense forms get our attention. Gradually and unconsciously, we become desensitized to higher and higher levels of violence until only really serious events get our attention. In this way, violence sneaks into our lives. The process is so subtle, we don't even realize it's coloring our own thinking and behavior. And that's scary.

Because we've all become desensitized, we all face a huge challenge in learning to see violence with fresh eyes. When you set out to examine how much violence is a part of your daily life, you'll need to look very closely. Chances are, you'll be surprised at how desensitized you are and how much violence has become acceptable to you. With fresh eyes, we can recognize even the small acts of

violence when we see them and take action. We get our new eyes by discovering the lessons we've consciously and unconsciously learned about violence. Let's take a look at a few of the most powerful ways we learn the lessons of violence.

Lessons from Family Violence

"Family, the group to which most people look
for love and gentleness, is also
the most violent civilian group in our society."

— Murray Straus, author of *Behind Closed Doors* —

For better or worse, most of us learn at home much of what we know about getting along with others, solving conflict, and managing anger. Whenever individuals with all their different needs and desires share a small space, frustrations are inevitable. But different families handle conflict in different ways. And no family is perfect. When someone has a bad day, it's easy to take it out on those who are closest, and that often means family members.

In many families, parents unknowingly teach their children to be violent through their own behavior. When parents swear at the TV, yell at people in traffic, drive aggressively, kick animals, slam doors, fight with each other and storm out, express racial hatred, or are mean and sarcastic, the message is not lost on young people. That message is that aggressive or violent behavior is acceptable.

Parents who explode in rage, threaten violence, or use physical intimidation to control family members teach their kids that aggression is the best way to gain power over others and settle disputes. If children are allowed to yell, scream, destroy each other's

> "My parents are divorced and sometimes they fight. When they fight, I start to feel really bad and like it's my fault."
>
> — Jonathan, 13

Describe a time you experienced violence in your family.

▶ *My 15-year-old sister had come home from a concert an hour later than her stingy 10:00 P.M. curfew. My dad had been drinking that night and was enraged at the fact that his daughter was home late. They cussed back and forth while my brother and I stood back and kept our mouths shut.*

• Mary, 16

When I was younger, my mother had an abusive boyfriend who hurt me and my brother physically and mentally.

• Rukahs, 14

My mum was a very aggressive person because she was alcoholic and addicted to drugs. When she'd come home with her boyfriend, they would get into a fight and then they would take it out on me. As a result, I hate most things in life and the pain is just sitting there waiting till I get really angry and then I am the abusive one.

• Kashe, 16, New Zealand

My dad has a very bad temper. He has been mentally abusing me for most of my life. I have a mountain resentment for my dad that will probably never leave me because of it. We fight whenever we get together.

• Jamey, 16

things, or fight, the message from parents is that kids get what they need in life by using violence.

> "My father has an explosive temper. That's all you need to know."
>
> — Silverkat, 15

Because you've been desensitized, you may not even be aware of the degree of violence in your family and the lessons you've learned. Young kids constantly watch adults for lessons on how to be a grown-up. They learn what they see and automatically incorporate it into the person they're becoming. If you grew up with violence, then for you, it may feel normal. Unless you have role models outside the family who can help you see that some of what you learned about violence at home isn't acceptable, and help you discover new ways of acting, you may get into trouble later.

"Wherever you go, there you are."

— Ram Dass —

The next problem is that lessons about violence learned at home almost always go with us when we go to school!

Lessons from School Violence

Many schools are working hard to deal with violence. They publish rules about violent behavior and require violence awareness training for everyone. They offer classes on anger and conflict management, assertiveness training, and peer mediation programs. At these schools, educators and other staff are aware of the serious nature of all behaviors on the continuum of violence, and they respond with serious consequences for students who don't follow the rules about aggressive behavior. In this kind of a school climate, young people can feel safe and be comfortable reporting the violence they encounter, because they can count on adult support when they need it.

But there are still some schools where the people in charge aren't as effective in dealing with violence. If they see problems, they tend to ignore them because the challenge of dealing with school violence is complicated and difficult. As a result, every day many acts of subtle and not-so-subtle violence occurs in these schools.

In schools that haven't taken a stand against violence, it's common to find:

○ bullying and other aggressive behaviors

○ students blackmailing smaller, younger, or less popular kids

○ vandalism

○ pushing, bumping, tripping, and other aggressive acts

○ students fighting inside the buildings and on or near the school grounds

○ weapons

○ gangs that use physical force or intimidation to control others

○ cliques that wield power in the school

"Fifteen percent of students reported gangs present at their schools. Of these, 35 percent feared attack at school; 24 percent feared attack going to or from school."

— National School Safety Center —

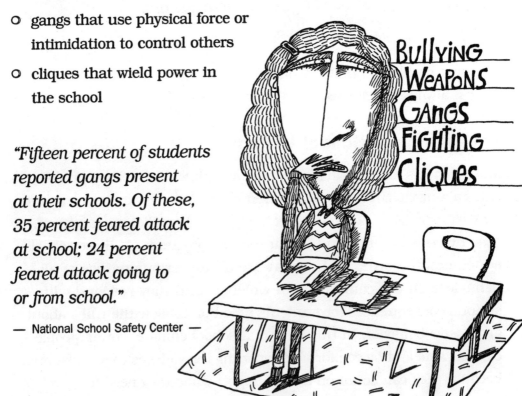

Bullying
Weapons
Gangs
Fighting
Cliques

"There's not a metal scanner or high-tech device that can accurately predict whether a youngster is going to commit an act of violence."

— Dr. Ronald D. Stephens, Executive Director —
National School Safety Center

Research on school violence tells us what most kids already know: where violence is common, it's very difficult to concentrate on schoolwork or relax. When people are fearful, they don't even want to go to school. One study by the National Education Association shows that every school day, 160,000 kids across the United States skip classes because they fear physical harm. That means that each day 160,000 kids don't learn, don't increase their chances of a better life through education, don't get to ask questions, don't get to participate in a sport or club, and don't get to be with their friends. It's a huge loss to them personally and to the communities that need them to become contributing citizens as adults.

In most schools, only a handful of young people are the primary trouble-makers. But because schools are desperate to do something about violence, in many schools *all* kids are put under surveillance, required to wear badges, go through metal detectors, and/or be constantly watched on video. "Everyone" becomes a suspect, and "school" begins to look and feel increasingly like a prison.

> "I learned about violence from my older brother and his friends at school. They would tell me to go hit or push someone around and back me up. At 14 I thought this was cool. Later when I would get mad, I'd use what I was taught and I fought a lot. It's not so cool now."
>
> — Nick, 17,
> Red Wing
> correctional facility

27

Do you feel safe at school? Why or why not?

> At school, I feel safe because I know that all the doors are locked and that no one there would be very violent. We have a system where you can't get into the building without a teacher who has keys to the doors.
>> • Elise, 12

> No, look at all the school shootings.
>> • Bebe, 14

> Yes, because I can trust my friends to help and back me up.
>> • Jonathan, 13

> No, because you never know what could happen when you get someone mad.
>> • JD, 13

> Yes, why should I not? Sometimes I'll get scared but I think, hey, the person will do it in or out of school. Why be afraid?
>> • Meg, 15

While these actions are sometimes justified, the lessons they communicate are that we don't know whom we can trust, we are all vulnerable, and we need to be on guard at all times.

When violence is unchecked, going to school means living in a climate of fear, not one of learning. In schools where violent acts aren't effectively addressed, kids learn other lessons, like how to pick sides, join the right group, or wear the right clothes in order to be safe. They also learn how to dodge bullying by going the long way home and that skipping school for a day means a little relief. Worst of all, they learn not to expect adult help. They learn that to survive in a violent environment, one has to be constantly on guard and always make the right choices.

Lessons from Community Violence

Like some families and schools, some communities are very violent. In the worst cases, gangs control the neighborhoods; shootings, drugs, and crime are regular parts of life. Violence or the threat of violence dominates the lives of young people and adults. In communities where violence is a way of life, the people learn powerful lessons about violence because their survival depends on it. They don't talk to strangers, don't make eye contact, and dress to avoid attracting attention. They learn to avoid certain parts of the community, to keep up their guard at all times, and to tolerate the sounds of gunfire and people yelling. It's like living in a war zone—people have to watch their every move to keep from putting themselves in grave danger.

> "I learned about violence from TV, the neighborhood, family, school, enemies, gangs, drug dealers, and addicts. Where I lived, there weren't consequences because the police didn't care or were sick of it. But if you did get busted, the consequences are correctional facility, jail, or prison."
>
> — Jacob, 18, Red Wing correctional facility

> "There was violence in my community on a daily basis. There were fights, gunshots, stabbings, and other forms of violence packed into the small neighborhood I lived in."
>
> — Samuel, 16, Red Wing correctional facility

If you've always lived in this kind of community, you've probably been desensitized to the violence around you. You may be unaware of how much fear, being on guard, and violence you call normal. You may have unconsciously learned to accept the life-destroying feelings of anger, hurt, hopelessness, and the uncomfortable sense of injustice and constant vulnerability.

Even those who live in communities with much lower levels of violence experience a mild degree of background fear. People have learned to lock the house and car doors, avoid certain neighborhoods, react cautiously when strangers talk to them, and be prepared to summon help in a hurry. Almost everyone has learned to feel a little scared and vulnerable because of the violence in our communities.

> "I feel safer in the after-school program at Golden Eagles [Native American Center] than where I live."
>
> — Kristina, 13

How do you

feel about

the violence

in your

community

or in ones

you've heard

about?

I feel totally bad for the families of all the victims where there have been shootings.

- Jon, 14

My neighbors fight really loud. It sucks.

- Lowell, 13

Being a graduate of Columbine, I would say that everyone is a little more paranoid about everything. It really has made a difference in me, though. I view life in a completely different way, and I definitely treat people with more respect. I try to enjoy my life in every aspect and try not to focus so much on the bad things.

- Dessie, 19

I think it's sick that gangs kill people for material things. If people wanna be in them, fine. If they wanna kill people, let them kill their own and rivals, not the innocent ones.

- Tiny, 16

It doesn't bother me unless it's happening to me or a friend.

- Grant, 13

Lessons from the World around Us

An enormously powerful source of lessons about violence speaks to you every day, saying violence is okay, violence is normal, violence is fun, violence isn't dangerous. This voice says that violence is what you need to solve problems, be respected, and be a hero. Sounds crazy, but those messages are being presented to you every day of your life.

Through television, music, movies, computer games, newspapers and magazines, some sports, and even billboards, we absorb messages that teach us lessons about violence. If you're looking for the ways you have become comfortable with violence, your daily media consumption is a good place to start.

"Television should be a way to entertain, educate, and teach our kids how to grow, not a way to teach them how to shoot to kill."

— Senator Ernest (Fritz) Hollings, South Carolina —

Television

Television, which most of us have been watching all our lives, is a very powerful source of lessons about violence. You may be surprised at just how many lessons this little box has fed into your life.

○ *Television shows.* Any night of the week, you can find killings, guns, and fighting in television shows. Violence is the core theme of police and detective programs, many made-for-TV movies, and talk shows. Shows let you "ride along" in police cars to real crime scenes, go with a paramedic to an accident, shooting, or domestic violence scene, or watch victims of violence get patched up in hospitals. In sitcoms and variety shows, you hear people use

Do you think that violence in the media contributes to aggression in young people? Why or why not?

Yes, it's kind of a monkey-see-monkey-do world out here.
- Alejundro, 16

I believe that the media contributes a fair amount to violence in young people because the young people see all the attention the people who commit crimes are getting and want that same attention.
- Steve, 10

Yes, because what you put in is what you get out. If you put violence in, that's what will come out.
- Holly, 17

Yes, definitely. I studied how violence in the media affects people. It can cause concentration to be thrown off after viewing, irritability, and not to mention a more violent person.
- Nicky, 14

No, violence has existed way before the media. If you're stupid enough to do something that the media shows, you're stupid enough to do something violent anyway.
- Seary, 17

sarcasm and make fun of people to get laughs. Even the educational or history channels show programs with graphic violence from past wars, the lives of criminals, and natural disasters.

Considering how many TV shows are based on violence, it's no surprise the American Psychiatric Association reported that young people in the United States will have seen 16,000 simulated murders and 200,000 acts of simulated violence on television by the time they are eighteen.

○ **The news.** Every day the TV (and radio) news brings you stories about murders, shootings, accidents, or other violence in your community. The global news covers wars, bombings, accidents, natural disasters, and other kinds of violence. Gruesome color pictures of those who've been injured or killed often accompany TV news coverage.

> "The world today is so used to seeing violence on TV, in newspapers, and in computer games that we have all become numb to it."
>
> — Holly, 17

With so much reporting about all the bad/sad/violent events, we are led to believe that violence is the most important thing happening. When you think of all the really wonderful things going on around the world, it seems that way too much of the news has become stories of violence and tragedy. When we're exposed to all these violent images and stories day after day, unless they're really shocking, they don't bother us anymore, and eventually we pretty much quit reacting to them.

> **"Take more violent programs off TV and teach kids from birth that violence is wrong."**
>
> — Peter, 17

○ *Cartoons.* Even when little kids watch cartoons, they are learning lessons of violence from television. Because it's so easy for parents to use television or videos as an electronic baby-sitter, many children are exposed to innocent-looking violence at a very young age. In many cartoons, cute characters are hit, kicked, squashed, pushed, run over, and even shot. These violent images are accompanied by artificial laugh tracks and exciting music. These early lessons of violence are sugarcoated to appeal to little kids. Some cartoons are just violence with training wheels.

> **"Growing up, I always watched cartoons. When I watch the cartoons now, I cannot believe the violence in them. For example the Bugs and Daffy cartoon when they are arguing about whether it is rabbit or duck season. Elmer shoots Daffy in the face and the only thing wrong with him is his bill gets knocked to the other side of his head."**
>
> — Kat, 19

As kids get older, they move from cartoons to superhero programs. You can probably remember your favorite. These programs skip most of the cute violence and humor and become seriously violent adventure stories. The main characters almost always have to overcome an evil foe by using their superpowers, which usually results in some form of violence. The fast pace and special effects are exciting, but when you isolate the message—that aggression and power can solve problems—you can see that these shows teach some potent lessons about violence.

▶ **"Parents need to**
▶ **control more of**
▶ **what their kids**
▶ **are watching."**
▶ — Janine, 17

Music

Some bands and singers build their fame on songs that celebrate violence. Lyrics and images in music videos depict shooting the police, murder, or date rape. Some even suggest self-violence, like suicide and taking drugs. Lyrics sometimes demean women or men because of their gender and even encourage sexual harassment or assault. The intense images in music videos fly by so fast that you can't always tell you're being fed violent or sexual concepts. Because the rhythms can be so hypnotic, you may just lose yourself in the experience . . . and in the process, unconsciously pick up more lessons about violence.

Do you think violence in music is a problem?

I've experienced so much violence in music that I have gotten used to it. But music that makes violence against women look unimportant or okay makes me upset.

• Kari, 17

Music when they talk about worshipping Satan and suicide upsets me.

• Chris, 17

In some music they talk about women as bitches and how they beat and cheat on them.

• Jessica, 18

In a lot of rap songs and some punky kinds of music, they really go into detail about killing people. It's sick.

• Nicole, 16

In a song on the radio a guy rapper was singing about stuff like rape, stuff like that. It's very inappropriate for the radio or anywhere.

• Lynette, 13

Last year after a concert I went to, I saw a huge line. I thought it was the bathroom, but when I got to the front it was the injury line to a nurse.

• Pam, 14

"For the last three decades, the one predominant finding in research on the mass media is that exposure to media portrayals of violence increases aggressive behavior in children."

— American Psychiatric Association —

Movies

Many movies contain graphic violence. They show people being maimed, wounded, or killed in an incredible variety of ways. The action is compelling, the special effects unbelievably good, and the music hot. But violence or the threat of violence is still at the core of the experience. In most action movies, even the "good guys" depend on violence that's totally unacceptable in real life. When the hero uses violence to save the day, the message we get is that violence is acceptable, especially if you're on the "right" side.

Computer Games

Computer games are another common source of violent images and simulated acts of violence. Many games contain gory visuals, weapons, blood, and flying body parts. You hear the sounds of characters being shot, hacked, hit, or otherwise toasted. The voice of the enemy often teases or taunts you to provoke your anger or stir revenge. Players try to get more powerful weapons and endless ammunition to stay alive. When you watch people play these games, you often see the fear, aggression, and the feelings of power on their faces as they struggle to destroy the enemies.

> **"Nothing surprises me anymore. Film, TV, and music are becoming more and more violent. They keep pushing the limit and making new rules. Soon, we'll actually be seeing more murder, rape, stealing, and abuse."**
>
> — Tabitha, 17

Sometimes players, caught up in the action, actually talk violently to the game screen.

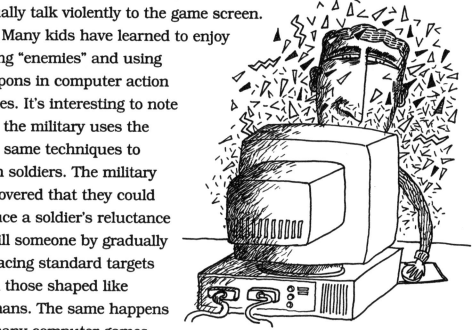

Many kids have learned to enjoy killing "enemies" and using weapons in computer action games. It's interesting to note that the military uses the very same techniques to train soldiers. The military discovered that they could reduce a soldier's reluctance to kill someone by gradually replacing standard targets with those shaped like humans. The same happens in many computer games as technology allows more realistic action and characters. If people old enough to join the military can be desensitized to violence in this way, it can have the same effect on younger kids too.

> *"When playing these video games, a child actually holds a gun ... and points it at a screen to shoot the 'enemy,' thereby exactly mimicking the techniques used by military trainers to prepare soldiers for combat."*
>
> — James Garbarino, Ph.D., author of *Lost Boys* —

Newspapers and Magazines

In the daily newspaper, just like with television and radio news, you can get information on the latest assaults, auto accidents, robberies, rapes, and shootings. The national and international news sections bring you the most violent events in your country, as well as

Do you think

that violent

computer

games make

kids more

aggressive?

I believe that violent computer games increase the likelihood of violent actions towards others. The person gets so used to the killing—it becomes so normal that they just don't care anymore.

• Steve, 10

It is cool because I would never do it in real life, and it is interesting to see what mass murderers go through.

• Jamey, 16

I do play fighting-type video games. What I like is being able to work out any fighting fantasies I have in a safe manner, as opposed to taking them out on a real person.

• Jessica, 18

I think they are just fun. Most of them are strategy, and I like that. But I have to admit that it wouldn't be the same without the bad guy yelling and getting blown into bloody chunks when you kill him.

• Justin, 17

I'm surprised that you can shoot someone's head off in a video game.

• Maria, 16

information and images covering uprisings and natural disasters around the globe.

Many news magazines also contain gruesome photos of violent events. Unlike the images in television news broadcasts, which disappear after they've flashed across the screen, these photos stick around. At home, in a rack in the grocery store, and even in your doctor's or dentist's office, you can pick up a magazine and see haunting photos of people killed in car bombings, police actions, wars, and earthquakes.

> "I think a major kind of violence is with girls thinking that models from magazines, who are very slim, are what guys find attractive. There are many girls my age who look very good but feel that they are fat. I know this is because they compare themselves to those models."
>
> — Raja, 15

Even fashion magazines contain violence. By portraying only perfectly dressed, beautiful people in articles and advertising, they are suggesting what we should look like in order to be acceptable. The conspicuous absence of people with different body types, people from different cultures, and people with different kinds of physical challenges is really a subtle form of social violence. It's like a powerful clique telling everyone else they don't belong based on how they look or dress.

Some Sports

If violence is defined as "any mean word, look, sign, or act that hurts a person's body, feelings, or things," some sports are very violent. Most sports require players to use protective equipment and have referees who keep things from getting out of hand. These measures protect both the players and the crowd from the violence built in to these activities. In most school sports, excessive violence is kept in check. But in many professional sports, barely controlled violence appears to be a major purpose of the game.

o *Boxing.* The goal of the sport is to punch harder than your opponent. The boxer who does the best job of beating up the other wins.

o *Professional wrestling.* This "sport" is really a theater of violence complete with stories of rage, hate, cheating, and revenge. Wrestlers brutalize opponents by hitting, kicking, stomping, and slamming them against corner posts. Fans enjoy the fierce rivalries scripted for the wrestlers.

o *Hockey.* Players must wear helmets, mouth guards, and body padding to protect themselves. Slamming opponents into the boards, pushing, and tripping are considered normal, and bloody, gloves-off fighting isn't uncommon.

o *Football.* Huge men slam into each other with the hope of sacking the quarterback, tackling the ball carrier, and preventing a touchdown. Severe injuries are common.

> "I think violent guys in sports get looked up to by kids. It's not good but they make a lot of money."
>
> — Okugn, 10

> "I'm always surprised about the violence in wrestling. I know it's fake and for entertainment but I was shocked."
>
> — Sarita, 16

○ *Sports reporting.* The language of sports coverage reflects the language of war. Winners annihilate, beat, crush, roll over, or destroy their opponents. These sound-bite descriptions emphasize the violence built into the sports.

In all these sports, violence is marketed as entertainment. But even when activities are closely managed to prevent injury, people get seriously hurt, tempers flare, opponents and fans express anger and rage, and the desire for revenge is raised to irrational levels. The crowds yell and scream for more, the play-by-play announcers narrate the violence, and the advertisers make big money. Through it all, we unconsciously learn to hurt someone when we're angry, to yell at people, and to get revenge when we've been hurt. We learn that you need to be strong, aggressive, and violent to survive and be a winner.

Getting New Eyes

No one escapes the powerful influences of these lessons of violence that color our thinking and behavior. Exposure to these lessons makes it easier to respond violently in a quick moment of anger. While you may have enough skills to limit the intensity of your response, in an unguarded moment you, too, may become a contributor to the violence in the world.

Once we understand how these lessons of violence influence us, we've begun to make the violence visible. When we can see these messages about violence with fresh eyes, we can begin to make better choices, choices that will ultimately make our world less violent.

The lessons of violence from the world around us are a bigger problem for the most vulnerable among us. These are the young people who also learned the wrong lessons in their families, schools, or communities. The most vulnerable kids don't have some of the necessary skills and lack critical connections to supportive adults. When they become isolated, stressed to their limits, and filled with anger, resentment, and hopelessness, they are at high risk for exploding with rage. In those moments, all the lessons of violence seem to them to justify aggressive actions, and the smallest event can turn them into human volcanoes.

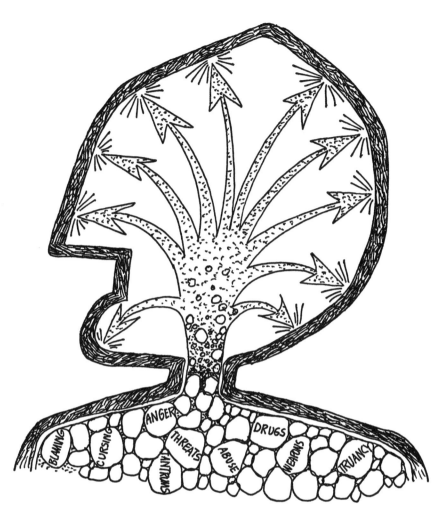

CHAPTER 4

The Human Volcano

People are always amazed when a person explodes with some intense, irrational act of violence. It's especially hard to understand how young people can be so filled with rage, resentment, hopelessness, or desire for revenge that they'd become an explosive human volcano, killing others or taking their own lives.

But underneath every young human volcano is a story of hurt and pain, and a person without the skills and support network needed to deal with uncomfortable feelings.

Why Kids Explode

Let's say it takes one hundred things right in a life for it to work smoothly. Most kids have a lot of things right and lives that work reasonably well. When you have a good share of the positive things in your life, it's easy to take them for granted. Things like strong self-esteem, some really great friends, and trusting relationships with an adult or two. You may also take for granted your ability to understand and express your feelings. You probably have the ability to express anger in reasonable ways and to get through conflicts with some degree of success. In addition to all these assets, you might even have the benefit of having a nonviolent and supportive family, school, and community environment. Having all these things working in your life helps protect you from becoming a human volcano.

Most young human volcanoes are really people just like you in that they need to feel loved and to feel that they are a part of things. They feel pain deeply and get angry when people are mean to them. In so many ways, they're average young people. But they may have a seriously troubled family background, their sense of self-esteem might be damaged, or they may lack skills necessary for relating to others. They may be without the important, supportive connections with people in their families, schools, and the communities where they live. Another thing is certain: they always have a very hard time dealing with their angry feelings in nonviolent ways.

Because of the trail of hurt and pain that's left after human volcanoes explode, it's tempting and easy to say these people are sick or evil. But the truth is that in so many ways, a lot of these young people have made numerous attempts to reach out to others in some way or spent years trying to make their lives work. With so little right and very little support, however, they're like the miners' fragile canary. They are extra-sensitive to the messages that say violence can solve problems and release your big and angry feelings.

Predicting Human Volcanoes

It's almost impossible to tell who will explode and who won't. What makes prediction difficult is that the unique and complicated mix of factors that cause any one individual to explode varies considerably from person to person. Human volcanoes can come from different kinds of family backgrounds and have very different personality types. Some do really well at school; some do poorly in their classes. They can be popular or not, and they may or may not be part of a clique. Some like violent computer games and others don't. While most troubled young people either talk about their feelings or behave in ways that indicate they need help, some give no visible warning at all.

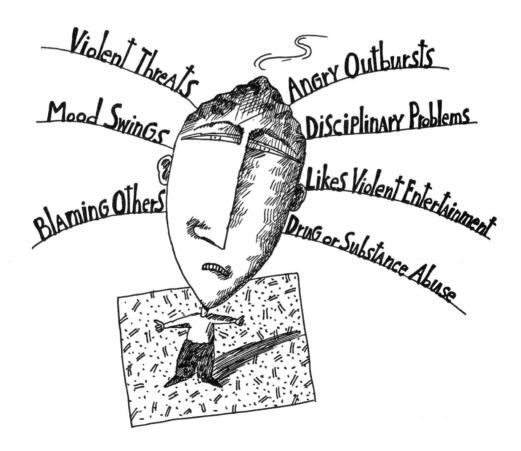

Do you know anyone who you think could be a human volcano?

I know a few people who are walking time bombs. They are constantly in the midst of fights, pain, and terror. These kids don't like to talk about their feelings and keep them bottled up.

  • Tabitha, 17

Yep! They make me feel that they can snap and not know how to control their anger. They have a mean look to them.

  • Amy, 17

Yes, a friend of mine is like that. When you're around these kinds of people, you have to be careful what you say and do. It makes me feel like you have to watch your every word, which is scary.

  • Lydia, 17

My cousin used to be so violent but now he's not. But he's always tense, so I feel if you push his button, BOOM!

  • Bobo, 16

The Secret Service, the federal agency that protects the U.S. president, has interviewed kids who have exploded at school and killed students and staff. Agents are looking for patterns that predict the potential for extremely violent behavior. But even their work has not provided an accurate way to predict who will become a human volcano. They've discovered that some of those they interviewed wanted to die and hoped they'd be killed in the act. Some wanted attention, while others told researchers that they tried to blend in and didn't want to be identified. But the bottom line is that their research and that of others hasn't provided a formula to accurately predict who will become a human volcano.

"It would be so much easier if all the people who did this [explode with violence] dressed weirdly or were outcasts."

— Robert Fein, forensic psychologist —

Characteristics of Human Volcanoes

While the research doesn't provide a way to predict with any certainty who will explode, it has given us information on characteristics shared by many human volcanoes. The National School Safety Center, which has tracked school-associated violent deaths since 1992, has come up with the following list of behaviors and conditions that are common to people with the potential to harm themselves or others. Remember that the following list just describes common characteristics; it doesn't predict behavior and it's not a guilty verdict. People at high risk for injuring themselves or others with violence:

○ has a history of tantrums and uncontrollable angry outbursts

○ characteristically resorts to name calling, cursing, or abusive language o habitually makes violent threats when angry

o has previously brought a weapon to school

o has a background of serious disciplinary problems at school and in the community

o has a background of drug, alcohol or other substance abuse or dependency

o is on the fringe of his/her peer group with few or no close friends

o is preoccupied with weapons, explosives or other incendiary devices

o has previously been truant, suspended or expelled from school

o displays cruelty to animals

o has little or no supervision and support from parents or a caring adult

o has witnessed or been the victim of abuse or neglect in the home

o has been bullied and/or bullies or intimidates peers or younger children

o tends to blame others for difficulties and problems s/he causes her/himself

o consistently prefers TV shows, movies or music expressing violent themes and acts

o prefers reading materials dealing with violent themes, rituals and abuse

o reflects anger, frustration and the dark side of life in school essays or writing projects

o is involved with a gang or an antisocial group on the fringe of peer acceptance

o is often depressed and/or has significant mood swings

o has threatened or attempted suicide

If You Think You Could Explode

Some readers of this book might find that the list of characteristics put out by the National School Safety Center seems to describe themselves. They may feel like they are on the edge of exploding in some dangerous way right now. If this is you, you should know some things before you do anything.

You Need Support

You need to know that you are *always* responsible for your actions, even though you may not know how to deal with your problems in nonviolent ways. You need support to help you understand why you're feeling so angry, frustrated, and hopeless. You probably don't have the skills you need to deal with your big problems and complicated, uncomfortable feelings. Many people feel like exploding, but they learn they don't have to hurt others as a way to deal with that feeling.

> **"At certain times violence seems the best answer, but**
>
> **it isn't. I chose violence and paid tremendously. At**
>
> **the time of my last offense [breaking and entering],**
>
> **I paid about $3,000 and spent fourteen months locked**
>
> **up. It's a lot for a 17-year-old. So when you feel like**
>
> **being violent, THINK! It works—it did for me. I stop**
>
> **and think every time I get mad, and now I'm an A and**
>
> **B student, family life is great, and I'm not in jail.**
>
> **Just THINK!"**
>
> — Garrett, 18

You may not yet have some of the important coping skills and support you need (and deserve) to help you meet all the challenges that are a natural part of a young person's life. But that doesn't mean it's okay to blow up.

Instead, make a much more self-loving choice. Find help to learn healthy ways of getting what you want and need. Using violence to do so will *always* make your life worse. You need and deserve someone to be there for you.

Violence always comes with a price, and a prison sentence may be only part of the cost. Think about facing a life of losses, regrets, sad friends, families in pain, burnt bridges, unhappiness, isolation, being without friends, and long-term legal consequences ... just for starters.

Anger is temporary, but you may face the consequences for life if you explode.

It Can Get Better

No matter how pressurized with anger, hurt, frustration, and thoughts of revenge you feel, you can get help. If you reach out in time, your life can get a lot better, and you can discover better ways of dealing with your feelings and actions.

> "I got into a fight just to help my friend a long time back. I kicked that dude in the face and beat him down because he was messing with my friend. I got in big trouble I'm still payin' for, and I still feel bad today years later."
>
> — Josh, 17

Remember, you are not unique in feeling the way you do. Many people have difficulties and lives that seem unfair, unjust, and cruel. Most of us feel lost, confused, and isolated at times. Many people want to lash out to relieve the hurt they feel inside. Some people have felt this way for hours or weeks, and others have lived with these uncomfortable feelings for much, much longer. You are not alone in your feelings.

But countless young people have learned their way out of feeling so bad and developed positive ways to deal with anger. Whenever people get together in a setting where there is enough trust to talk truthfully about feelings, they learn how people are really very much alike. Reaching out for help and getting support is the only path to a life that works. With a little self-understanding, compassion for others, and skills to help you deal with your feelings in positive ways, you can have a great life.

People Do Care

You may feel so bad that you think no one could ever understand you or would even want to listen. It may even feel like no one truly cares about what you're going through, but it's just not true. Let me repeat that: *It's just not true.* This kind of thinking, which comes out of isolating yourself from others, will only magnify your problems.

What's closer to the truth is that because you're so consumed with anger, self-pity, and thoughts of "showing them," you're withdrawing from all the people in your life who'd be there for you in a minute, if you'd just reach out. Some of the people around you may be busy and distracted; some may have even rejected you in some way. But somewhere, probably very close, is someone who does care and can help you. It may take a little work on your part to find that person, but that effort is always easier than the monumental challenge of rebuilding a life that's been destroyed by violence. The big question is do *you* care enough about *yourself* to search someone out, and do you have the courage to ask for help?

I care about you. All the people who contributed to this book did so because they care about you. We've all taken our time to share our thinking and experiences in the hope you wouldn't feel alone.

FAMILY TRUSTED ADULTS SUPPORT GROUPS BEST FRIENDS CRISIS LINES TEACHERS POLICE

We all hope you'll find the courage to keep reaching out until you get the help you deserve. We know you're worth it.

You Can Get Help

Asking for help is a sign of emotional health, not of weakness. When you know you're up against more than you can handle, it's smart to ask for help. It may take courage to tell someone that you're scared of what you're feeling and thinking. But if you had a serious gash in your leg, you probably wouldn't have too much trouble going to the emergency room and asking for help. Feeling like you will hurt yourself or others is a similar kind of wound. This wound also deserves attention, and there are people willing and able to help. Be strong, smart, and self-loving enough to reach out.

If you're having trouble thinking of where to turn, here is a list of people who can help. Start at the top of the list and keep moving down until you've found someone you can trust. Tell that person what's going on with you and ask for support and help.

o your immediate family

o other adults in your extended family

o your best friends

o any adult at school you trust

o your friends' parents

o support groups or adults in school or your place of worship

o any adult you trust at a youth center

o adults you trust in your neighborhood

o hospital emergency rooms

o police and fire departments

o crisis hot lines

Please keep trying until you get someone's attention. Your life is too precious to waste. Besides, we need your help to reduce the violence in the world.

Describe

a time you

felt so angry

you wanted

to hurt

someone.

Once my friend Cody stole something from me so I totally trashed his room.

• Paul, 14

I got really mad when I saw my little brother walking with dirty shoes on the clean carpet. I got really mean and start yelling at him. When he started crying, I stopped and felt bad about myself.

• Elizabeth, 16

I feel like that all the time.

• Tiny, 16

Once when I was at a beach with my little brother, he destroyed a sandcastle that I'd worked hard to make. I yelled at him and threatened to destroy his beloved Game Boy. He stayed a hundred feet away from me for the rest of the day.

• Tizzle, 12

When the doctor said my brother is dead.

• Lowell, 13

When my uncle wouldn't stop pushing me.

• Jon, 14

Making a Difference

While most young people have many things right in their lives, every-one is missing some of what it takes to have a perfect life and to be the best possible person. As a result, we all have moments when we experience mini-eruptions—when we are mean and hurt others in some way.

If we are going to do something about violence in our world, we'll have to learn how each of us can be less violent and what other actions we can take to make a difference. It's true that you won't single-handedly stop wars, stop the sale of guns, stop violent gangs from forming, keep people from exploding with anger, create safe communities, stop violence in the media, keep weapons out of schools, keep people from bullying, or stop violence in families. This is the big stuff that requires lots of committed people, all working together and taking a big-picture approach to the issues.

But as a motivated individual, you can do many things. You can start with the things you have control over, like your own thinking and behavior. You can also look at how you handle yourself in your relationships with family, friends, and all the other people in your life. You can explore what you can do to make a difference in your school, community, and even in the world at large.

Imagine the impact if each of the many thousands of people who read this book do just a few things to reduce violence. Like water that continuously drips on a stone and eventually wears it away, the actions of many people, each doing what he or she can, will reduce violence in the world. The second part of this book is filled with specific ways you can be a major player. The world needs your help; let's go for it!

Part 2

What You Can Do to Reduce Violence in Our World

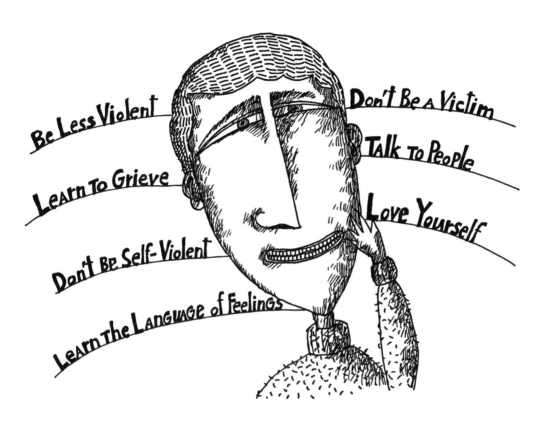

Be Less Violent

Don't Be A Victim

Learn To Grieve

Talk To People

Don't Be Self-Violent

Love Yourself

Learn The Language of Feelings

CHAPTER 5 What You Can Do for Yourself

The best and easiest place to begin to reduce violence in the world is where you have the most control. For most of us, that means looking at our own behavior, considering how our beliefs and actions have been influenced by all the lessons of violence, and then doing the things we can to change. This chapter explores ways we can change our behavior to have a significant impact on reducing violence.

Don't Be a Victim

If after learning about different forms of violence, you realize that you are being victimized, take some action. Violent people believe their behavior is okay when people don't take a stand. Report bullying, threats, or any form of violence directed toward you. In taking action against serious violence, you have to be very careful. Dealing with people who are violent is scary and often flat-out dangerous. Facing these people alone gives them the upper hand. That's why in almost every case, you must find someone to tell, preferably an adult. Find a family member, a teacher, a counselor, someone from your spiritual community, or someone you trust and ask for help. (Turn to the list on page 54 for more people who can help.)

If you're in immediate personal danger, don't be afraid to call a crisis hot line or even 911. You'll find phone numbers for getting immediate help listed inside the front cover of your phone book. The people who answer crisis phone lines have had special training, really care about you, and have loads of resources at their fingertips. They can provide information on things like emergency shelter, counseling, and support groups. If the violence is happening while you're in school, you must tell a teacher, counselor, or school

> "Outside of my family,
> the band director
> from school has
> always been there
> for me. I feel secure
> with him because he
> listens with all his
> heart and has never
> let me down."
>
> — Maggie, 17

social worker. *You are not alone.* There are lots of people out there who understand what you're going through and are willing and able to help you. But it's up to you to reach out.

By taking a stand against the violence, you'll be doing your part to make the world a safer place for yourself and for others. Dare to stand up for what's right. Do it for yourself first but also do it for those who are witnesses, who in their own way are victims too. Don't put up with violence in any form; take some kind of action—you're worth it!

Be Less Violent

Another way to reduce violence in the world is by making sure your own actions aren't violent. This is where you have the most control because you make the choices about how you act. It sounds simple, but it's not always easy. It would be nice if you could just say, "Starting today, I'll never be even a little violent again." Well, you could say it, but it would be almost impossible to do. Our lives have been so influenced by violence that we almost automatically slip into aggressive thinking and acts. But you can decide to work at being less violent. You can commit yourself to learning how violence plays out in your life and to doing a better job of behaving nonviolently. The fact that you're reading this book is a giant step in that direction. The next step is to understand your own choices and behavior.

Understanding Your Potential for Violence

If you're setting out to make nonviolent choices, the first challenge is to better understand yourself and to see the violence that may be hidden in your current choices and behaviors. The following questions are designed to help you get to know yourself better. As you answer these questions, you'll get a clearer understanding of how violent influences are working in your life.

HOW DO I RESOLVE CONFLICTS? DO I THINK ABOUT REVENGE?

DO I LIKE VIOLENT COMPUTER GAMES?

DO I WATCH AND LISTEN TO VIOLENT ENTERTAINMENT?

DO I LIKE TO PICK ON YOUNGER OR WEAKER PEOPLE?

The goal of this exercise is to help you see your behavior with fresh eyes so you'll be better prepared to make nonviolent choices.

o In your family do people resolve conflicts by fighting? Is hitting okay? Are yelling and other forms of intimidation acceptable? Do stronger individuals pick on weaker ones? Do people use sarcasm or mean jokes about family members? Are the females treated differently than the males?

o Did the toys you played with as a child include weapons or action figures of violent superheroes? When you were a little kid, did the shows you watched on television have violent content?

o Do your role models in real life, movies, television, or books exhibit violent behaviors?

o Do you go to violent movies, watch violent television shows, or listen to music with violent words? If your choices aren't obviously violent, do they contain subtle violent messages?

o Do you like computer games where you can blow away your enemies with some type of gun or weapon?

o Have you ever picked on people younger, weaker, or less powerful than yourself? Do you have friends who are bullies?

o Do you belong to a clique that actively excludes others? Are criteria such as popularity, music preferences, clothing styles, hair color, ethnic origin, or neighborhood important for membership in your group? By discriminating in these or other ways, do you let people know that they are not acceptable and not wanted?

o When you have a major disagreement with someone, do you get really angry, yell, or think about ways to get revenge if you don't get what you want?

o Have you ever hit, pushed, or kicked someone with the intent to hurt him or her?

o Have you ever intentionally damaged someone else's things?

○ Do you write about violent things or about getting revenge?

○ Do you hang out with people who talk about guns and hurting others in some violent way? Have you ever planned acts of violence or revenge?

A lot of "yes" answers to these questions means that violent influences may have increased your potential for violence. Becoming aware of your potential for violence is the first big step toward being less violent.

Becoming Less Violent

Once you become aware of the ways you tend to use words, looks, signs, or acts that hurt a person's body, feelings, or things, you can choose to do things differently. In the process of learning to be less violent, you'll get the satisfaction of not adding to the meanness in the world. You'll also avoid the personal pain and self-destruction that violence always generates. Best of all, your life will become more enjoyable. People will feel safer around you, which means that you may have more and even better friendships.

"Friendship with oneself is all important,
because without it one cannot be friends
with anyone else in the world."

— Eleanor Roosevelt —

Don't Engage in Self-Violence

Another important way to reduce violence in the world is not to be violent to yourself. If you look closely, it's amazing how many of us treat ourselves really badly. Using the definition of "any mean word, look, sign, or act that hurts a person's body, feelings, or things," you'll be surprised how you or people you know commit self-violence.

Do you know

any people

who are

violent and

successful?

Would you

like to be

like them?

One girl who is popular is kind of violent. If you do anything to her, she'll just really get mad and sometimes explode. I wouldn't like to be like her because people like that make you not really want to hang out with them.

• Norma, 16

Many male athletes have been accused of being violent in the past yet they still get paid big money.

• Kari, 17

Professional wrestlers, but I wouldn't want to be one.

• Grant, 13

I do not know violent and successful people, but see them portrayed in movies.... I don't want to be like them ever.

• Florian, 10

Understanding Your Potential for Self-Violence

Here are just a few examples of self-violent behaviors. See if any of them have crept into your life.

○ *Destructive self-talk* is a way we can injure ourselves. Do you call yourself stupid or an idiot, out loud or in your head, when you make a mistake? Talking to ourselves like this eats away at our own self-confidence. If someone else talked to you that way, you'd probably feel hurt or angry. You might lash out or just walk away. If you heard someone calling another person ugly or fat, wouldn't you feel uncomfortable? Talking to yourself like that can have devastating effects.

Do I Practice Destructive Self-Talk? Perfectionism? Drinking And Drugging? Physical Injury?

○ *Perfectionism* is a self-defeating way of thinking where you feel that whatever you do, no matter how hard you try, no matter what obstacles you overcome, and even regardless of other people's positive view of your performance, you just don't measure up. A little voice in the perfectionist's head says, "What's wrong with you? You should be able to do better." No matter how well you've done, it's not good enough.

How would you feel if you had just worked really hard to finish a cool project for school and a friend said it really sucked and could have been a lot better? What if someone said negative things about almost everything you did? How do you feel about people who always put you down or point out your imperfections?

Would you keep a friendship with someone who just couldn't see anything really great about you? Perfectionism is just like that, and it's serious self-violence. Never letting yourself feel good about who you are is a powerful way to slowly self-destruct.

○ *Drinking or using other drugs* is another way to inflict violence on yourself. Using chemicals that can make you sick, give you diseases, destroy your brain cells, or impair your thinking so you put yourself in risky situations is major self-violence. Abusing substances means snorting, shooting, or smoking anything; drinking; or taking pills that damage your body or your brain. You may as well just take out a hammer and hit yourself on the head.

Using alcohol and other drugs puts you at a much greater risk for violence. When your thinking is impaired, you're more likely to commit violence *and* be a victim of violence. For example, here are some sobering statistics about alcohol use from the U.S. Department of Justice:

▸ "People can be violent to themselves in many ways, whether it is drug use, cigarettes, alcohol, or even food overindulgence. However, I think many of these people can't control it and secretly wish they were strong enough to overcome their problems. They should just ask for help."

— Jessica, 18

- 41 percent of convicted violent offenders report that they were drinking at the time of their offense
- 41 percent of all traffic fatalities are alcohol related

Plus, use of drugs, including alcohol and tobacco, is illegal for minors. In addition to any legal consequences that you may encounter if you use, you face another major risk: addiction. When you are addicted, the substance you use causes changes in your brain chemistry so you need to keep using it, even when it's screwing up your life. Your brain develops until the age of 21, so if you begin experimenting with tobacco, alcohol, or other drugs before that age, you're much more likely to get addicted.

o *Physical injury* means literal self-violence. Examples include deliberately cutting yourself or scarring your body in some way. This also includes the dangerous practices associated with eating disorders that alter your body chemistry in damaging ways. Acts such as driving recklessly, playing with guns, or fighting physically are high on the list of aggressive behaviors that often lead to serious self-injury. Then there is suicide, the ultimate form of self-violence, the total waste of a life that could have made the world a much better place.

> **"I used to slit my wrists whenever I got upset. I thought**
> **that the pain would stop me thinking about why I was**
> **upset because I would think about my sore wrists and**
> **not think about my anger. I stopped because my friend's**
> **mum committed suicide by slitting her wrists and I didn't**
> **want it to happen to me."**
> — Mel, 14, New Zealand

Choosing Self-Love

You may be tempted to be self-violent because the world around you is a mess in some way. Unlike people who erupt outwardly with violence when they are angry, hopeless, and confused, self-violent people turn their reaction inward. Whatever the reason, self-violence is wrong and a signal you need some objectivity about yourself and your life.

When you choose any form of self-violence, you also hurt the people who care about you. It's painful to feel helpless while you watch someone you love self-destruct.

The world is violent enough without you being violent to yourself. You can choose self-love over self-violence by caring about yourself, being nice to yourself, and respecting your body. When you're in enough pain to be self-violent, it can be very hard to reach out for help. But the most self-loving and self-respecting thing you can do is to find someone you trust and say, "I'm scared because I'm injuring myself and I think I need help to quit." Once you take that first important step, things can get better and the next steps will be easier. If you want to stop violence in the world, start with yourself because you are worth it!

> "When people don't love themselves they begin to do hurtful things to themselves. I had a friend who was so insecure and loathed herself to the point that she inflicted pain on herself by carving into her arms with knives and other objects. She found herself ugly, but really she is the kindest, sweetest person."
>
> — Kari, 16

Learn about Loss and Grief

Much of life is made up of loss and grief. We feel loss when we realize that how things used to be has ended. Loss is the event that changes things, and grief is the process of working through your feelings about the loss. We have big losses, like when a friend or family member dies or when parents get divorced. We experience loss when friends move away or when we change schools. It's a loss when violence shakes our sense that we are safe in the world. Other types of loss include things like being cut from a team, being excluded, being let down by a friend, or losing something you liked.

Loss is a normal part of life, but a part that people don't like much because big feelings get stirred up. The bigger the loss or the greater the number of losses in a life, the bigger and more complicated the feelings. Anger, resentment, frustration, hopelessness, confusion, and a sense of unfairness are some common and even healthy emotions people experience when they are grieving a big loss.

People who understand the grieving process and have support can work through these feelings without injuring themselves or others. Healthy grieving can lead to better self-understanding and maturity. Sadly, the experience can be disastrous for people who don't understand what they're feeling, don't have the language to express their emotions, or don't have supportive people to help. A person so over-whelmed with grief emotions can become lost in negativity, anger, and hopelessness to the point where the crazy feelings of self-destruction and the desire to hurt others almost make sense.

Did you ever experience a loss that made you angry?

I was adopted, and sometimes I get so angry that my mom had put me in an orphanage I yell at her.
  • Kate, 11

Yes, when my dog had to get put to sleep. I was mad because it happened to me.
  • Jonathan, 13

I was crushed by my brother's death. I'm angry because he's gone.
  • Lowell, 13

One of my grandpas died and that made me very sad and extremely mad because I didn't get to tell him that I loved him. I didn't get to say good-bye.
  • Lynette, 13

My father was an alcoholic controller and seriously depressed. I hated that he wouldn't allow himself to be a better man, father, and husband. Now he is gone and I still am angry that I couldn't have a father to love or be loved by.
  • Tabitha, 17

Learning to Grieve

Big and small losses will be a part of your life. You can try to deny grief or pretend to the outside world that you don't have feelings about your losses, but the grieving will go on inside you nonetheless. That's why it's so important to learn how to work through your losses without hurting yourself or others.

Learning that there are predictable stages that people go through when healing from loss can make your recovery easier. You'll see how the feelings you experience are normal (even if they're not comfortable) and fit into the healthy grieving process. Healthy grieving also means that you learn how to express your difficult feelings in constructive ways.

Because grieving is a complicated topic, learning about the process takes time and requires the help of knowledgeable people. You can take some of the steps below to learn about loss and grief and how to support people who are grieving.

> "Since the divorce, my mom always looks like she's going to explode, but she holds it in. She gets mad a lot and is crabby a lot, but she doesn't take it out on us."
> — Kelsey, 16

○ **Read a good book on the subject.** *Help for the Hard Times: Getting through Loss* is a great book on the subject written especially for young people. This book teaches you about the predictable stages in the grieving and healing process and what people can do to take care of themselves along the way.

○ **Talk to people who have been through a major loss.** Ask them what the grieving process was like for them, what feelings they had, and how they're feeling now.

○ **Attend a grief or loss group.** You can find these groups in your school, at a place of worship, or at a hospital. These groups will help you to learn about what's normal during the grieving process and how people heal from losses.

○ *Write down your feelings.* When you're experiencing a loss, keep track of the specific feelings you have and when you have them. That way you'll begin to understand your own response to loss and how the predictable stages of grieving appear in your healing process.

○ *Talk with family members.* Ask someone in your family to tell you about your family's traditions around loss and grief. Many families follow a set of rituals designed to help them deal with the loss and feelings of grief when someone dies.

People can grow in self-understanding and maturity by learning to deal with losses in healthy ways. One very important skill for healthy grieving is learning to speak the language of feelings. Not having the ability to speak this language is a primary reason people become human volcanoes.

Learn the Language of Feelings

Without knowing the language of feelings, people are not aware of what feelings they're having or what caused them to feel the way they do. They also don't have the ability to measure the intensity of their emotions and the impact of their feelings on others. Basically, they're operating without some crucial information. To these people, big feelings are experienced as something very uncomfortable going on inside them that they don't like, can't explain, and don't know how to handle.

When people with a limited emotional vocabulary are faced with difficult personal problems, they have very few options. Filled with a confused jumble of feelings and physical sensations, some choose isolation and wish that people would "just leave me alone." Some do their best to function normally, but

▶ **"I believe that people**
▶ **who start most of**
▶ **the violence are**
▶ **kids who have**
▶ **trouble expressing**
▶ **themselves in any**
▶ **other way."**
▶ — Tommy, 16

72

inside the emotions churn and grow and at some point they lash out at the world in a futile attempt to release the internal pressures. But neither of these choices—escaping inside yourself or exploding—is ever the way to solve their problems, and soon the pressures begin to build again.

Without a language to express your feelings, you're very much like an infant with all kinds of hurts, needs, and wants but no way to communicate them to others. All a baby can do is cry, scream, kick, and throw things to get attention. Those around the baby have the challenge of trying to figure out what's going on and guessing at what will help. People who haven't had the opportunity to learn the language of feelings lack the ability to communicate what they're experiencing,

> "There used to be this kid in my class who, whenever he got mad, would throw things around and sometimes hit others. I think he did that because he was so frustrated and didn't know how else to express his feelings."
>
> — Lillian, 16

what they want, or how they hurt. They are especially vulnerable to the messages that it's okay to use violence to deal with uncomfortable internal feelings. Learning the language of feelings opens up lots of new possibilities.

Speaking the Language of Feelings

As you learn and begin to speak the language of feelings, some amazing things happen. You become more clear about what you're feeling, and you can distinguish one feeling from others and even give it a name. When you're angry, sad, hurt, or lonesome, you'll experience and understand each of those emotions differently. You'll also be better able to gauge the intensity of your feelings. This means you'll be aware that you feel stronger about the death of your dog than you do about having a friend cancel a date. With more emotional "information," you can link the feeling to the cause and talk about what you're experiencing in ways that allows others to understand.

Some of this may sound elementary to you, but many people aren't taught these skills. They go through life frustrated and uncomfortable and, as a result, sometimes get in trouble. But even those who have the gifts of emotional understanding and expression can benefit from growing their feelings vocabulary.

"Lacking an emotional education, a boy meets the pressures of adolescence ... with the only responses he has learned ... the typically 'manly' responses of anger, aggression and emotional withdrawal."

— Dan Kindlon and Michael Thompson,
authors of *Raising Cain: Protecting the Emotional Life of Boys* —

How to Grow Your Feelings Vocabulary

If you were raised in an environment where feelings weren't expressed or talked about in positive ways, you might not have much of a feelings vocabulary. But remember, *all people have lots of feelings.* Feelings are part of life. It's just that some people don't have the language to understand or express what's going on inside them. But anyone can develop a feelings vocabulary with study and practice. When learning to speak any new language, some techniques work a lot better than others. It's no different with the language of feelings. Here are some things you can try.

○ *Get a good teacher.* Learning any language is easier if you have a good teacher, someone with lots of experience speaking the language. It may take time to find someone who speaks the language of feelings, but you'll know it when you find the right person. Family members or other relatives might be a good place to start, but a counselor or another adult in your school are other possibilities. Someone in your neighborhood or spiritual community you trust can also be an emotional teacher.

You'll learn a lot just by hanging out with people who are good at expressing their feelings in positive ways. If it feels comfortable and you trust them, you may even want to talk about how you feel about the hard stuff in your life. The important thing is to get involved in the world of feelings.

O *Learn the words/link the feelings.* When you start to learn a new language, you typically begin with a few common words. The same is true for the language of feelings. Pick a few basic emotions: sad, excited, confused, hurt, happy. Develop an interest in *just* two or three emotions. When people around you have these feelings, pay attention to the tone of their voices, the look on their faces, how they behave, and how they interact with others. You'll find that some ways of expressing feelings work better than others in helping people get their needs met.

Emotional moments are common at funerals, weddings, and victory celebrations, when people are arguing, at birthday parties, or when friendships break up. These occasions always involve big feelings. If you're paying attention, you'll have lots of chances to study people expressing feelings.

o *Use feelings language.* As your skills develop, take every opportunity to express your feelings. Because you know more about feelings, you're more likely to recognize the best moments. When someone stops and asks, "How ya doin'?" take a moment to see what you're feeling, and then actually say it. When someone asks, "How do you feel about this?" you can share your thoughts and then add the feelings that go with them. For instance, "I think it was mean for him to push me into the locker. I feel angry and a little scared." The more you use the language of feelings, the easier it will be for people to understand you. Who you are and what's going on inside you will be clearer, not only for you but for others too. But that's just one of the many gifts that will come from speaking the language of feelings.

The Gifts of Speaking the Language of Feelings

Here are some of the benefits of becoming more skillful at expressing your feelings.

o *Relief from the dark side.* Feelings of general discomfort, uneasiness, and pent-up frustration begin to go away when you express your feelings instead of holding things inside. When the ability to express feelings is limited, *all* feelings are limited. That means the positive feelings are held back too. But as you express your feelings more openly, you get to experience more upside feelings, like happiness, silliness, excitement, and love. You're liberated to experience more emotions of all kinds, including the good stuff!

o *Self-understanding.* The more you study your emotional life, the better you will know yourself. As your emotional vocabulary

Who can

you share

your feelings

with?

▶ *The person I feel closest to is an older
friend. I can call him anytime, talk
about anything, and he always understands. The reason I trust him so much
is because he has never judged me for
anything I've done.*
  • Chris, 17

▶ *My friend's mom. She's really cool.*
  • Tom, 14

▶ *I can share my feelings with this
woman at my church because she
is always there to listen and cry with
me. She understands me.*
  • Red, 17

▶ *I don't have anyone!*
  • Lowell, 13

grows, you will become increasingly aware of what a complex and
interesting person you really are. Compare the way two people
watch a basketball game. One spectator knows only that getting
the ball through the hoop to score points is a good thing. The other
is a total basketball nut. This person follows the sport and understands what each player is doing, the reasons for the referees'
calls, and the coaches' overall strategies. The game is much more
interesting to the serious basketball fan. When you learn about
something, you see it differently and can appreciate it more. In the
same way, as you learn more about your complex emotional life,
you (and others) will begin to understand and appreciate *you* more.

○ *Satisfied needs.* Not only will you understand yourself better, but you'll also do a better job of explaining what you want to others. You'll be clearer about what you need and better able to ask for it directly. While you won't always get what you want, clearly communicating with others about your needs is much more satisfying than having tantrums no one else can understand.

○ *Connection with others.* Because your feelings language is more descriptive, more of who you are inside shows on the outside. People will know how you feel, how important something is to you, what you really want to do, and how much you like or don't like something. People can connect with you more easily because they have more opportunities to say, "I feel that way too," or "Hey, we have that in common." There is more of you for others to connect with and more opportunities for people to see you as a person they want to get to know.

> "Last summer my two best friends got really angry with
> me because of something I did. They said they couldn't
> be friends with me anymore because there was no trust
> in our friendship. I knew I couldn't lose them as friends,
> so I tried my hardest and I gained their trust back."
>
> — Kelsey, 16
>
> "Trust is a feeling where you understand and know someone
> so well that you depend on them for anything. Trust comes
> when you have spent a lot of time getting to know them
> and their personalities and even know how they think. You
> know when you can trust someone—maybe not right away,
> but you will."
>
> — Elise, 12

○ *Intimacy.* Many people are lucky enough to have a really special friend. These kinds of relationships only evolve over time. They are built on trust and sharing, and they can't be rushed. People who can share their feelings have a stronger bond than people who just talk about the weather, homework, or football scores. When you trust someone enough to share your big feelings and that person shares back, you have a really deep bond.

○ *Choice.* One of the best gifts of learning to speak the language of feelings is that you get to decide what you want to do about how you feel. As you learn to recognize feelings, experience them individually, and talk about what you're feeling, you have a wonderful opportunity to decide what to say, what to do or not do, and when to act. You get more control of yourself and your life. Choosing what to do about how you're feeling is more effective than going around feeling dark and being moody and occasionally exploding in a violent, angry overreaction. Choice means having feelings instead of feelings having you.

> "There are a lot of things I am more than angry about but I don't want to burn myself inside out from anger. That's why I'm learning to manage my anger. When you're out in the world, your positive options are infinite. But when you're in here and you're angry, it's too late. You're just a locked-up angry person and that's it."
>
> — Dwayne B., 21, New York correctional facility Locked up since 15

When you've examined how your own thinking and behaviors may influence you to be violent, you're ready to consider the next set of challenges: What you can do to reduce violence in your relationships with others.

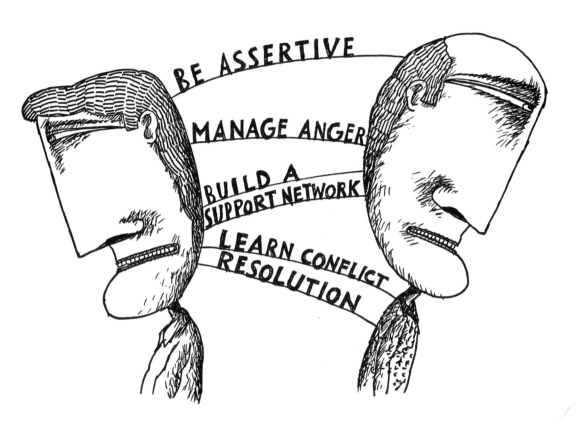

BE ASSERTIVE

MANAGE ANGER

BUILD A SUPPORT NETWORK

LEARN CONFLICT RESOLUTION

CHAPTER 6 What You Can Do in Relationships

When complicated problems and feelings are stirred up as a result of differences between people, it's easy to get mad and raise our voices, or even to explode violently. When people are violent, feelings are always hurt. Sometimes people stay hurt for a long time and waste a lot of energy thinking of ways to get revenge.

Differences between people are a normal and predictable part of life. In fact, conflict can be good because working through disagreements improves our relationships. But in order to benefit from our differences, we need to learn some new skills. The ability to express our anger constructively, to ask for what we want firmly and directly, to resolve conflicts peacefully, and to empathize with others all reduce the potential for violence.

Because many parents don't have good relationship skills, kids don't see these skills being used. As a result, many young people are left on their own to figure out what to do when problems occur in their relationships. But even a little training in relationship skills helps you make your way through this complicated and sometimes dangerous territory. Let's take a look at some of these skills and how you can use them.

End the Circle of Violence

Violence moves in a circle that begins with a violent behavior and is fueled by the desire for revenge. In your own life, maybe even recently, there may have been a time when you got so mad, you wanted to get revenge for the way someone behaved toward you. If you acted on those feelings, you kept the circle of violence alive.

> "If you are violent to someone, then they will be violent back more times than not. And then you will want to retaliate. That's why it just needs to end with you, or it never will."
> — Johnny, 16

It all starts with the violent behavior, but to stop the circle of violence we have to say no to our desire for revenge and decide that the violence stops now, here, with us. To learn how to do that, we have to take apart the whole violence drama and look at its components.

The Violent Behavior

The circle of violence starts with the violent behavior—"any mean word, look, sign, or act that hurts a person's body, feelings, or things." It can be a serious crime or an unintentional insult. It's hard to know what can set off anger in another person, but when the violent behavior inspires the desire for revenge, the circle has begun.

> "If *you* don't start it, there will be nothing to finish."
>
> — Josh, 16

Feelings

Victims of violent behavior always experience feelings. Some people may not show them or, if they don't understand their emotions very well, they may not realize what feelings they're having or be aware of the intensity of their reaction. When people feel they've been mistreated, they commonly experience sadness, anger, disappointment, anger, fear, anger, a sense of betrayal, anger, loss of trust, anger, embarrassment, anger, frustration, or even ANGER. Most people who've experienced violence get to anger pretty quickly, and along with anger often comes the desire to retaliate.

The Choice Point

The choice point in the circle of violence is extremely important. The choice point is the time right after the violent behavior and before the response. It's that moment when a person can choose between escalating the violence or healing.

Sometimes this point occurs in a flash, and at other times you have months or even years to think about your response.

People without anger-management skills often find themselves so physically and emotionally involved, so filled with anger and hurt, that they just want to get revenge in some way—NOW. They don't even realize they have a choice but blow right past this important decision point and go directly to revenge. In doing so, they also pass up the opportunity to end the negativity and avoid all the other costs of being caught up in the circle of violence.

> "Think about what effect you may produce with your actions and words. I used to be a semi-violent person, and, trust me, it doesn't get you anywhere but down."
>
> — Nicky, 14

Revenge

Revenge means "payback," "getting even," hurting a person in some way after that person has hurt you. People may choose to get an "eye for an eye" by returning the same act of violence, or they may find some other way to get revenge. Like control of the ball in basketball, the choice point goes back and forth among the people involved in the circle of violence. Unless someone decides to choose healing, one violent behavior leads to the next, which leads to the next and the next. People talk about "getting even," but people engaged in a circle of violence aren't staying even—they're getting sucked down into the dark hole of revenge. And if they go down far enough, they can create problems that will follow them for a lifetime.

> "Violence locks you in the past and eats up your insides rehearsing plans to get even. It's a sickness."
>
> — Kareem, 17, correctional facility in Texas

Healing

The key to breaking the circle of violence is to choose healing rather than revenge. You'll need both emotional self-understanding to not let your feelings control you and self-esteem to take the nonviolent path toward healing. It's not always easy to stop at the choice point, but it's always worth the effort. Your decision to turn toward healing doesn't mean that others will do the same. But when you choose to step out of the circle of violence, *you* are healed. You find relief from the anger, hatred, and resentment that churn inside you when you're lost in thoughts of revenge. You move toward self-caring, self-respect, and freedom.

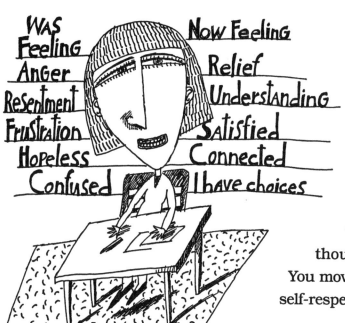

People who choose the path of revenge are responsible for their actions. Given the serious costs of being engaged in a circle of violence, you'll make an important investment in your life when you learn the skills necessary to tame the powerful anger monster and make self-respecting choices.

> "You should see that it won't do any good to try to get back at someone. You really only hurt yourself by doing it."
>
> — Roy, 16,
>   Red Wing
>   correctional facility

Develop Anger-Management Skills

Anger is a difficult, complicated, and powerful emotion to experience and it takes skill to handle it in positive ways. The feelings behind anger can be some combination of hurt, frustration, surprise, sense of injustice, resentment, fear, desire for power, vulnerability, betrayal, or many other emotions. Because there are so many feelings involved and because we're all so different, it's almost impossible to know why someone gets angry.

Anger is such a troublesome emotion that some people just pretend they don't feel it. These people try not to acknowledge or express their anger in any way. But the angry feelings are still there and they pile up inside. Holding in anger is kind of like holding your breath—you just can't do it forever. It takes serious physical and emotional effort to contain all the big angry feelings. That's why psychologists tell us unexpressed anger can be a factor in serious physical and emotional illnesses like depression, high blood pressure, headaches, ulcers, and even some types of cancer.

People who say they don't ever get angry are prime candidates for becoming human volcanoes. Sometimes the person you'd least suspect, someone who's always nice, just can't hold the anger inside any longer and pops, releasing huge amounts of ugliness at the people nearby.

On the other end of the spectrum are the people who are angry at almost everything but don't try to hold it inside. They are so filled with angry feelings that any little thing can set them off. Often—and sometimes without their knowing it—these people speak forcefully, argue at the drop of a hat, or use threatening

▶ **"Usually I'm pretty**
▶ **nice, but when I'm**
▶ **really mad, I swear**
▶ **a lot at the person**
▶ **or at things. I throw**
▶ **things around, or**
▶ **sometimes I let**
▶ **out my anger by**
▶ **punching things or**
▶ **kicking."**
▶ — Liz, 16

Describe

what you do

to keep from

exploding

when you're

REALLY angry

about

something.

I spend time by myself. And pray. Both help me focus on the problem rather than my anger and help me stay calm and rational.

• Kelsey, 16

I go somewhere quiet or away from people and have some time to myself to think about the situation rationally and from both sides of the situation.

• Rebecca, 16

I run up to my room and lock the door. I put the music on and go to bed.

• Strawberry, 16

I think just biting your lip and turning your back is always the best thing to do, but it is extremely hard at times.

• Kirk, 14

I go to my room and have a chill time till I cool down.

• Zova, 16

I count backwards from twenty.

• Natasha, 17

I write poetry or I just write in my journal.

• Grace, 16

I think about the consequences and how I would feel afterwards.

• Kristin, 16

gestures. They may feel sorry afterward, but because they don't know how to handle the big angry emotions, they have trouble preventing their outbursts.

Given these two very different relationships to anger, you may be surprised to learn that anger is a healthy, normal, and even necessary feeling. All the feelings behind anger are neutral, neither good nor bad. Feelings of anger are simply emotional information that tells us that we've experienced a real or perceived injury. We're lucky to have these feelings because they tell us we need to do something. But deciding what to do about anger is the tricky part. One thing's for sure, though: suffering quietly or having ugly outbursts are not the best way to go through life.

> ▶ "Sometimes a person
> ▶ has a bag of rage
> ▶ in them and it can
> ▶ be opened with one
> ▶ smart remark. Then
> ▶ there is a violent
> ▶ backlash, which
> ▶ can be verbal and
> ▶ sometimes physical.
> ▶ I personally have
> ▶ never been physically
> ▶ violent but verbally
> ▶ plenty of times."
> ▶ — Haciem, 16

Anger-Management Assessment

If you're going to reduce violence in the world, understanding your style of dealing with anger is a good place to start. The statements below cover a variety of possible responses to anger. Does one or more of them sound like your typical response to anger?

o I never get angry.

o If people never got angry, the world would be a wonderful place.

o When I'm really angry, I don't show it until I'm alone and can hit, throw, or break things.

o If someone is angry with me, I get angry right back.

o I don't like to be angry with others, so when I have those feelings, I distract myself by using alcohol, tobacco, or other drugs, playing violent computer games, focusing on food, or studying.

- The first hint I have that I'm really angry is that I explode with rage.
- I don't really get angry, but sometimes I cut myself or hurt myself in other ways.
- If people don't understand why I'm angry, it's their problem.
- It's okay to hurt people or their things so they really know how mad I am.
- If people make me angry, they are responsible for the consequences.
- Serious violence is the only way to express myself.
- People don't know I'm angry unless I lash out violently. It's bad to keep emotions inside.

If you said that *any* one of the responses above sounds like you, you're set up for some form of personal problems or damage in your relationships. That's why developing anger-management skills is the best hope for avoiding self-destruction from either keeping your anger inside or exploding with violence. People who know they're angry, who can stop before they react, and who can choose the best response for the moment have the best chance of responding to their angry feelings in healthy, nonviolent ways.

"I was at my baseball game when words between me and a kid from the other team were exchanged. Things escalated, and before I knew it, we were throwing fists."

— The Kemist, 16

The Skill of Anger Management

Managing anger doesn't mean you don't get angry. Anger management means you learn to recognize when you're angry and then choose to express your feelings in a way that has a good chance of making the situation better. Even a little training in anger management can make a huge difference in how well you get along with others and how you'll feel about yourself.

A healthy response to anger requires three things to happen in a pretty predictable sequence. This series of specific steps will allow you to go from the first uncomfortable sensations of anger to a positive outcome. First, you have to get a handle on your angry feelings, then accept responsibility for how you feel, and finally make a conscious choice about the best action to take. Let's look at these steps in a little more detail.

1. Get a handle on your anger. If you're going to manage your anger, you first have to know you're angry. It's easy to automatically respond to some real or perceived injury with an intense reaction before you have even realized you were angry. Your anger may seem to come out of nowhere, but if you look very closely, you can usually find the signs that a storm is brewing. Your thoughts and some powerful physical sensations are two reliable indicators.

- Angry thoughts. If you pay close attention to your thoughts prior to an angry outburst, you may hear yourself thinking about how unfair and wrong *they* are, how wounded you are, or even how you're going to get revenge. Your angry thinking is driving physical reactions and getting you ready to take action.

- Physical sensations. When we feel threatened, a set of predictable physical reactions called the *fight-or-flight response* gets kicked off. Your body reacts automatically and instantaneously to prepare you to run or fight.

Your heart rate increases and the blood moves from the center of your body to your arms, legs, and head so you feel hotter. Your digestion shuts down, so you may feel butterflies in your stomach and your mouth may go dry. Your hands and feet may sweat, your muscles tighten, and your breathing and heart rate speed up as you become ready for action.

When you're angry, what physical sensations and feelings do you have?

When I'm angry, my palms start to sweat, my face turns red, and I start to breathe irregularly.

• Chris, 17

I have to hit something really hard.

• JD, 13

When I'm angry, I just want to go beat someone. I don't like when I get like this. I yell and my feet shake. I just can't keep my anger in. Believe me, I let people know what I think.

• Meg, 15

Tension, heavy breathing, tightness in the throat.

• Casey, 17

I get real hot and my muscles get tight.

• Vamp, 18

I like to hit things or run up and down the stairs.

• Josh, 16

It's lucky for us that our ancient ancestors got very good at running or fighting when they were threatened. If they hadn't, they would have been lunch for some big animal and we wouldn't be around. But the fight-or-flight response lives on in us and fires up every time we feel threatened. These physical changes can happen when someone is yelling at you or when you're just imagining that scene. The more intense the real or imagined threat, the more intense the physical response.

So you have to be very careful in these moments. You have a chemical riot taking place in your body, and you don't want it to push you into behavior that you'll regret.

Once the danger signal goes off, you may feel like you just have to do something. It's what people do in that moment that can make the difference between a positive outcome and a big mess in a relationship.

2. Accept responsibility. Once you've checked in with your thoughts and physical signals and you realize that you're angry, the next step is to accept responsibility for your feelings. It's pretty tempting to blame other people for your anger, but that's just an attempt to shift responsibility for your behavior. Other people, events, or circumstances may have stirred the feelings in you, but your anger is yours and it's your responsibility. You may get mad because of what happens, but no one *makes* you mad. When you are willing to be responsible for your emotions and your actions, you are in a powerful position because you can choose positive responses to your angry feelings.

3. Make a choice. When you can choose your response to anger, you are in charge. You're no longer a victim at the mercy of other people, events, or situations. Choice means freedom. People in correctional institutions for committing a rash act of violence will tell you that having the ability to choose

▶ **"Outside forces**
▶ **aren't the problem;**
▶ **we are the ones who**
▶ **cause aggression**
▶ **in ourselves."**
▶ — Jenna, 16

your response to anger is to have real power, the power to prevent the consequences they've encountered.

Choice means that you get to decide where and when and how intensely you want to express your feelings. You can choose whom you'll be angry with, what you'll say, and the language you'll use. Choosing how you'll express your anger works better than exploding unpredictably. Having choice about your response to anger gives you serious power, but it's just one of many gifts that come with anger management.

> ▶ **"Think about what**
> ▶ **you're doing to**
> ▶ **yourself as well as**
> ▶ **others.... If you**
> ▶ **keep being violent,**
> ▶ **there will be major**
> ▶ **consequences at**
> ▶ **some point, like**
> ▶ **getting locked up**
> ▶ **or even death."**
>
> ▶ — Nick, 17,
> ▶   Red Wing
> ▶   correctional facility

Anger Management as a Gift

As strange as it sounds, anger offers many gifts to you and those around you. First, your anger tells you something is not right in your world and needs to be fixed. You can't always change the things you're angry about, but your anger helps you know where the problems lie.

Second, when you share your anger with another person in a constructive way, you show that you care about your relationship, even if you aren't happy with something that happened. It lets the other person know that you want to see if you can fix what's broken in your relationship. If you can work through it, the connection between you becomes deeper and stronger. If you can't find a solution, you may need to break some ties or change your relationship with that person in some way. That can be hard, but by listening to and trusting the emotional information your anger provides, you can be true to yourself.

Another gift that comes with anger management is that you earn the respect of others. You become known as a reasonable, fair, and safe person to have around. You also gain self-respect because you're not getting yourself into angry messes that drag you down.

Best of all, you don't walk around either bubbling over with resentment, fear, and hurt or stuffing your anger in order to keep everyone else happy.

Learning how to manage your anger is a great start in forming healthy relationships and reducing violence in the world. But things can get even better when you know how to tell others what you like and don't like, what you want, and where you stand on issues. To do all that in a way that respects other people's rights and feelings takes another powerful set of relationship skills called *assertiveness skills.*

Develop Assertiveness Skills

People who behave assertively share their feelings, thoughts, and needs in ways that are clear, direct, honest, and appropriate. If you're assertive, you express yourself in ways that are respectful of others and yourself. Being assertive is really the best way to go through life. It means that you don't have to cave in to other people's wishes, go along with the crowd, or use intimidation or force to get what you want. An important first step in developing these skills is to determine just how assertive you are right now.

Assertiveness Assessment

Think about how you'd respond if you were in the following situations. On a separate piece of paper, answer the questions "yes" or "no." Your answers will help you assess your degree of assertiveness.

O When a friend is very late to meet you, do you say that you're angry?

O If someone borrows money from you and "forgets" to repay you, do you ask for it?

O When you're a newcomer to a group, do you introduce yourself and start a conversation?

O Can you say no when a friend asks a favor that you aren't comfortable doing?

I can TELL someone when I'm ANGRY.

I can accept COMPLIMENTS.

I can say NO when it feels appropriate.

I can INTRODUCE myself to STRANGERS at a social gathering.

o Do you speak up for yourself when you feel you are being treated unfairly by a business?

o Can you tell someone who frequently interrupts you when you're talking that you don't like it?

o Can you say "No, I'm not interested" when someone offers you alcohol or if your boyfriend or girlfriend asks you for sex? If the person keeps asking, can you say you don't like being pressured?

o Do you say "Thank you" and not minimize the compliment when someone tells you how great you look?

o Do you speak up if a teacher or other adult is unfair?

People with assertiveness skills would answer "yes" to most of these questions. Standing up for yourself, asking for what you want, making sure your opinions are heard, dealing directly with people who are unfair or aggressive, and staying true to yourself—and doing so in a way that is firm but respectful—are all examples of assertiveness.

Three Ways to Not Be Assertive

If you don't have assertive role models or haven't been trained in assertiveness skills, you're like many people who are confused about what it means to be assertive. Without some training, it's easy to think you're being assertive when your behavior actually falls into one of the categories of nonassertive behavior: *passive, aggressive,* and *passive-aggressive.* Nobody fits completely into any one category all of the time, but most of us have developed patterns of behavior and more often than not fall into one of the categories. As you read through the following descriptions, see where your typical behavior fits.

▶ "There was a teacher at my school who'd often say things
▶ that would hurt or embarrass people in front of the class.
▶ I couldn't handle watching this happen and stood up to
▶ her. There was indeed serious conflict, but it did get sorted
▶ out. I think she saw that people were genuinely hurt by the
▶ things she said, and I realized that she didn't intentionally
▶ mean to hurt anybody."
▶ — KT, 19

Passive

People who behave passively feel a little insecure socially and see their feelings and needs as less important than those of others. They prefer to hang in the background and often go along with what others want. They want to avoid conflict because they think that will make people like them and help everyone get along.

> "Passive people make me want to motivate them because they just sit there and don't do anything."
>
> — Meg, 15

But passive people can be frustrating to be around because they don't contribute much. It's hard to know what they want, to know their opinions, or even to know what upsets them. As a result, passive people are often ignored and can be terribly lonely because they don't have many friends.

Some people who behave passively confuse *assertive* with *aggressive*. Because the last thing they want to be is "pushy," they avoid telling people how they feel. As a result, they don't get their needs met and live with mountains of internal hurts, stresses, and depression. They are targets for bullying because they don't stick up for themselves and because they tend to be loners. They don't like to be picked on, but they don't know how or are afraid to stick up for their own rights. Passive people can have pretty miserable lives.

> "When I first started at high school, this girl started spreading rumors about me. People would act different around me. I don't really care anymore, but at the time it really, really hurt and I was so mad I could have killed her."
>
> — April, 15

Aggressive

People who use aggressive behavior fear looking weak and try to dominate others to feel okay about themselves. They talk about themselves a lot and ignore other people's wishes, contributions, feelings, and rights. These individuals tend to use sarcasm, talk loudly, engage in gossip, and make fun of people who are weaker, smaller, passive, or vulnerable in some way.

> ▶ **"I just want to know**
> ▶ **what makes bullies**
> ▶ **so special that they**
> ▶ **think they run the**
> ▶ **world. I hate them."**
> ▶ — KJ, 16

People who behave aggressively may have others around them, but they develop few deep friendships. Instead, they hang out with other aggressive people who tend to be self-centered, or they attract groupies who are trying to avoid being picked on and who fake friendship out of fear. Aggressive people tend to confuse assertive behavior with weakness and prefer to demand or just take what they want. Their bullying and other abusive ways earn them the disrespect of others.

Passive-Aggressive

People who are passive-aggressive have figured out how to be aggressive in a passive way. It's really the worst of both worlds. Like all people who behave passively, they often go around full of anger because they seldom get heard or get what they want or need. But instead of being direct with their anger, they "get even," sometimes in subtle ways.

Say, for example, that you forgot to repay some money you borrowed from a friend. A passive-aggressive friend probably wouldn't say anything about the money but might be crabby or give you the silent treatment for weeks. If you asked what was wrong, you'd get a response like, "Oh, nothing." Many people who behave this way haven't learned the skills they need to be direct, so they go through life continually "getting even" when their feelings are hurt. Sometimes they don't even realize they're doing it.

Life around people who behave passive-aggressively is very crazy. You don't know what they really want or how well you're getting along. You often get a sense that they're unhappy about something, but you don't know what's wrong because the issue is never clear. Their indirect expressions of anger make your relationship with them complicated. Lots of little "inconveniences" mean you are confused and frustrated most of the time. Like both passive and aggressive behaviors, passive-aggressive behavior tends to keep people from getting close, so people who act this way have few real friends.

Formula for Assertive Behavior

Mastering assertiveness skills requires commitment, training, and practice. But a short course in assertiveness can be very helpful. Try the following formula the next time you need someone to understand your feelings.

1. **Make eye contact.** Make sure you are looking directly at the person, so you know you have his or her attention.

2. **Get agreement to talk.** You need the other person to listen, so make sure he or she is willing to have a brief conversation.

   Example: "Becky, I'm upset about something you said yesterday. Can we take a few minutes to talk about it now?" (If the response is "No, this isn't the right time," try to set up a time when you can have the person's full attention.)

3. **State the issue and what you want.** When you have the person's full attention, you can say what's troubling you. Describe what you're thinking and feeling about the issue. Don't bring too much emotional intensity into the discussion and don't make judgments about the other person. Keep your comments focused on what *you* think and feel.

   "Yesterday when you said Alicia was really stupid, it made me pretty angry. I was angry because I don't like it when people gossip and I wouldn't want you talking about me like that. I need to know you won't be saying negative things about me

or others when we're not around. Will you make me that
promise?"

4. **See what happens.** After you've described your position and asked for what you want, wait. Don't ask any questions or make any suggestions that can take the conversation in another direction. Sometimes when people get a direct, nonthreatening request, they will just agree. When the other person responds to your request, listen and make sure you really understand. Give your full attention, even if it's uncomfortable.

> *If Becky says, "Well I've heard you gossip plenty of times!"*
> *listen and really try to understand what she's saying. Don't*
> *respond until you've heard her and understand.*

5. **Repeat your request.** If the other person doesn't agree to your request, you may have to ask again. As you repeat your request, reflect your understanding of his or her thoughts and feelings.

> *"You're right. I'm not perfect. I know I've been a gossip and*
> *talked behind people's backs too. But I'm trying very hard*
> *to change myself, and I don't want to gossip anymore. Maybe*
> *we can help each other by agreeing not to gossip. Will you*
> *promise me that you won't say negative things about me or*
> *others when we're not around?"*

6. **Stay focused.** If the other person tries to cloud the issue or change the subject, calmly bring the discussion back to your request. If necessary, you can agree to talk about the other issues at another time, but keep this conversation focused on your request.

7. **End respectfully.** You won't always get what you want, even when you ask for it directly and respectfully. But when you behave assertively, the other person knows where you stand, and you'll feel good about making your needs clear. After you hear what the other person has to say, you may look at the situation differently and even change your position.

Another option is to simply agree to disagree and leave the topic open for discussion later. Whatever the outcome, try not to end your talk with angry statements and hurt feelings. Thank the person for being willing to go along with your request or for at least listening to you. Ending the discussion on a positive note keeps your relationship respectful and means the person will be more open to talk the next time something comes up. Even without agreement, you can end by saying:

> *"It's okay with me if you want to think about it for a while. If it's all right with you, let's talk again after the weekend. And by the way, I really appreciate your willingness to talk this over. Thanks a lot."*

Assertiveness is a way to stand up for yourself and to have your needs and viewpoint considered by others. It's not a way to manipulate people to get what you want. By avoiding passive, aggressive, and passive-aggressive behavior, you'll prevent a lot of frustration and open yourself to the many gifts that come with assertiveness.

> *"If a man stands for nothing, he'll fall for anything."*

> — Malcolm X —

Assertiveness as a Gift

Self-respect and the respect of others are some of the most important gifts that come from being assertive. When you speak up about important issues, you're staying true to your values. You are more real and honest with others. By expressing your thoughts and feelings in direct and respectful ways, you become a safe and interesting person for others to be around. When you tell others directly how their behavior affects you, it creates the opportunity to fix a piece of your relationship that is broken.

People who behave assertively are also more genuinely open to hearing from others. They're not afraid to be good listeners and work toward common solutions. In addition to assertiveness, finding common solutions to conflicts involves another set of skills that help people come up with positive solutions to disagreements. Conflict-resolution skills represent yet another way to reduce the potential for violence in your relationships.

Develop Conflict-Resolution Skills

There are thousands of ways people can get into conflicts with one another. Someone hurts you, ignores your feelings, damages or steals your stuff, picks a fight, makes fun of you, stands you up, or lets you down in some way. . . . The list can go on forever.

Because each of us is unique, differences of opinion and negative reactions to others' thinking or behavior are inevitable. Conflict between people is common—that's why we really need to learn how to work through differences. The only other option is living with big, unpleasant, unresolved messes between people.

Conflict Between People Without Resolution Skills

It's possible that you seldom have serious conflicts with others, but that doesn't mean you don't have strong feelings about your differences—it just means you try not to show your feelings. As we've just learned, passive or passive-aggressive behavior—not sharing your feelings, thoughts, and needs in clear, direct, honest, and appropriate ways—may mean that you are quietly storing your anger inside.

Stored-up anger sometimes shows up as self-violence or comes out as an explosive act of violence. This can start the vicious circle of violence and revenge. Learning to resolve conflict is the only way out.

Conflict-resolution skills help people work through differences to reach a mutually acceptable solution. You don't have to stay stuck in ugly disagreements that escalate in intensity. With a little skill, you can learn how to disagree with others, acknowledge your differences, and either find a solution or at least remain on friendly terms.

> **"Talking to the other person is a better way—more brave, mature way—to solve your problem."**
> — Sophia, 16

> **"Don't resort to violence. There are countless other ways to solve problems besides violence."**
> — Lukkas, 16

> **"Violence can happen really easily and people will get hurt. Just don't stay mad for too long. Make up, work it out, and stay friends."**
> — Jonathan, 13

Describe a

conflict you

had with

someone

and what

happened

as a result.

My girlfriend and I got into an argument. She hit me, and I just walked away to keep from exploding. The conflict got solved when she apologized, but it took a long time.

• Boo, 17

My father doesn't get along with his sister (my aunt), but I love her. When she was getting married, I wanted to go to the wedding. He said that if I went, he would never speak to me again. I went because that's what I felt was right. I have not spoken to him since that screaming argument. It really sucks to know that my relationship with him is at the level where he can give it up that quickly.

• Bailey, 16

I got mad when one of my good friends tried to go after a dude I liked. The conflict got solved by talking about it and then letting it go. Everybody felt a lot better afterwards.

• BM, 17

I almost always have conflict with my mom. It's always difficult to work things out with her because we're both stubborn. She also does the door-slamming thing if I say something she doesn't agree with. She tells me to get out and get out of her face. Usually I stick around until we apologize to each other because I can't stay mad long!

• Julia, 15

Five Steps to Resolving Conflict

To get through a serious disagreement, five steps have to happen, more or less in order. While at first this process may sound enormously complicated, it becomes easy with practice. Of course it helps if everyone involved knows how and wants to work through conflicts.

1. Make a choice to work toward resolution. Unless you work toward a solution, most conflicts end with anger and hurt feelings. To work toward a solution, you'll need to practice anger management, to step back from your intense feelings and think about what's happening. It can be hard to come up for air when all you want to do is be right, get your way, or get revenge. But once you step back from the angry feelings, you're ready to step forward toward resolution.

> ▶ "It's bad to be
> ▶
> ▶ violent, because
> ▶
> ▶ violence separates
> ▶
> ▶ people and puts
> ▶
> ▶ walls up that are
> ▶
> ▶ hard to break."
> ▶
> ▶ — Frank, 16

2. Get agreement from the other person to work through your differences. Even when *you* are able to do this, the other person might have difficulty unhooking from his or her emotions. If the other person won't agree to talk, resolution isn't possible. When people prefer to continue to stew in their own angry juices, the best choice is to walk away. But when each person is willing to listen to the other, you can go to step three.

3. Get clear and communicate. You have to know what you want to have happen as a result of your discussion—this means thinking beyond the desire to be right or just get your way. Think about what is behind your hurt and the emotional intensity you're feeling. This may take some time to do, but it's critical to be clear about your viewpoint and what you need to get things straight.

> "Just take some time to think before you do anything big. If you sleep on it, I guarantee your rage or feelings will tremendously lessen."
>
> — The Kemist, 16

Once you know what you need, you must express those needs with assertiveness. Remember, being assertive means that you communicate in a way that's direct, respectful, and *not* aggressive. One critical element in conflict resolution is to express your needs using language that won't make others any more mad or defensive than they may already be. During a conflict, knowing the difference between I-statements and you-statements can be very helpful.

You-statements tend to turn into attacks: "You have the brain of a clam. Have you been underwater all your life? If you can't see reality, you should just crawl right back into your dark, muddy hole." Statements like this may satisfy your hunger for revenge, but they do nothing to solve the conflict.

In an I-statement, on the other hand, you use the person's name to show respect and focus on how you feel as a result of what happened. Then, without casting blame or shame, you can ask for what you need for the conflict to end.

> *"Estaban, I got angry when you told my girlfriend I was interested in dating someone else. I was also hurt because I thought we were really good friends and it felt like you let me down. If you'd be willing to be honest and tell her you made that up, I'd feel better about you and our friendship."*

Once you've calmly expressed what you really need, you can go to step four.

4. Listen. For a conflict to be resolved, each person has to feel heard and understood. For this to happen, each listener has to know how to listen when the other is speaking. You may be surprised to learn that listening doesn't just happen, but it's an important skill you can learn.

The kind of listening that ensures mutual understanding is called *active listening*. This means listening with an open mind. While someone is talking, you're not busy in your head, forming an argument to prove he or she is wrong or stupid or just doesn't get what you mean. Most people aren't the best listeners to start with, and hearing someone's point of view becomes even harder when our emotions are bubbling. It takes practice.

In active listening, you show that you are listening by looking at the speaker. You nod and say things like "Okay" or "Yeah" to indicate that you're paying attention, but you don't interrupt. When the speaker is done, repeat what you heard. The speaker then clarifies what he or she meant if you seem to have misunderstood. Then, once again, repeat what you heard. Continue listening and repeating until the speaker feels you understood the message.

Then switch roles. Continue until each of you feels understood. Active listening means that you very clearly *understand* one another's position, not that you *agree* with each other. When you get this far,

▶
▶ **"While someone is talking . . . listen. No judging, wait until**
▶ **they are finished, no advice-giving, don't defend anything,**
▶
▶ **don't reject what you hear immediately, repeat back what**
▶
▶ **you think they said, nod to the person, "hmm-hmm" a lot,**
▶
▶ **and think about exactly what is being said. It's the most**
▶
▶ **wonderful gift you can give another human being."**
▶
▶ — Elizabeth M., 48

you've made huge progress—sometimes enough that each of you begins to feel better about the other. When everyone feels understood, you can go to step five.

5. Brainstorm solutions. After getting clear about each other's position, the conflict may go away because the whole thing was driven by misunderstandings. But if serious differences remain, the next step is to work together to find a creative solution that works for you both. You want a solution that doesn't leave an angry loser with hurt feelings and a desire for revenge.

But it's not always possible to come up with a solution that lets you both be winners. On those occasions where finding resolution to your differences is more difficult, you still have the following options:

○ *Get an objective opinion.* Find someone you both trust who is fair and a good listener. This person could be a peer mediator. (See "Become a Peer Mediator" on pages 139–141.) Just having someone else look at the issue from the outside might unlock the logjam.

○ *Let some time pass.* Sometimes the emotional intensity can hide important information and possible solutions. You can both decide that you've been understood, but there's no solution to your conflict for the time being, so you'll talk about it later. You might even set up a time to talk again.

○ *Agree that you aren't going to find a workable solution.* This means that you each feel strongly about your different positions. While sometimes this might mean that you lose a relationship, in most cases it just means that you disagree.

Conflict Resolution as a Gift

As you get better at these skills, more and more of what used to be miserable, no-win fights will have positive outcomes. You'll spend less time feeling hurt, misunderstood, and angry with people. You won't waste time and energy planning revenge. You won't avoid conflict out of fear and will be more comfortable taking a stand because you know how to work through differences of opinion. You can maintain friendships with people who have different thoughts and opinions. But most important, you'll feel better about yourself, and you'll gain the respect of those around you for your skills.

One way to deepen your conflict-resolution skills is to try to understand how someone feels. The relationship skill called *empathy* involves using your feelings vocabulary when listening to others.

Learn to Empathize

Having empathy means that you have a good idea of what someone else is feeling. You can relate to the person because you've been in similar situations and experienced similar feelings. Have you ever said something like "No wonder Tara is mad—I'd be mad, too, if someone stole my money"? If so, you'd be *empathizing* with Tara, because you'd have some sense of what she was feeling and can imagine how she'd react to what happened.

> "I had a conflict with my best friend over 'he said/she said' stuff. We were at it for two weeks. One day we saw each other and decided that it was a crazy thing to be arguing about. We both cried and made up. That was five years ago, and today nothing can tear us apart."
>
> — Fonda, 16

As your emotional vocabulary grows, your ability to understand others' feelings also grows. You can understand what it means emotionally for someone to have parents divorce, to be bullied, or to be cut from the team. You'll know how sad, scared, angry, disappointed, or hurt another person can feel. Even if you haven't experienced the exact same thing, you can use your emotional imagination to make a good guess about what it's probably like.

▶ **"Put yourself in their**
▶ **shoes. How would**
▶ **you feel?"**
▶
▶ — Kelly, 16

You can know information about people—what they like to eat, what music turns them on, and where they like to hang out—but that's not empathy. Empathy means you know how they *feel* about their food, music, and hangouts. Empathy is "feelings knowledge." The more you know about how people feel about things, the better you understand them. The ability to empathize, to experience life through another's feelings, is a critical skill in relationships.

People who are prone to violence are pretty self-centered. They tend to focus on how they've been wronged, what's wrong with everyone else, and what they'll do to get revenge or feel powerful. They don't think about the impact of their actions on other people's lives.

Imagine what other people might be feeling or experiencing

On the other hand, people who can empathize with others are less likely to be aggressive or mean because they have a sense of what it would be like if it happened to them.

Empathy is a powerful tool for reducing violence in the world.

Developing Empathy

Growing your ability to empathize comes from paying attention to others. You can practice empathizing by doing some of the following:

○ *Listen for the language of feelings.* Develop the art of listening for feelings language or guessing what feelings are behind what people are saying. This is a great way to begin to tune in to the emotional part of another person. You may only be guessing in the beginning, but this activity will make you more aware of feelings and, in the process, make you a much better listener.

○ *Look for the physical signs of feelings.* You can learn a lot through people's body language and facial expressions. Try seeing if what they are "saying" with their bodies fits with the feelings they are talking about. Do people talking about sadness look slumped over, tired, and have their eyes cast down? Do people who are talking about being happy look strong, upright, bright-eyed, and open? Learning to match the physical "language" with the feelings it expresses is another way to understand what other people are experiencing.

○ *Imagine what other people might be feeling or experiencing.* When you use empathy, you say to yourself, "If I were that person, what would I be feeling right now?" You actually pretend to be someone else! With this kind of practice, your emotional imagination will get more fine-tuned.

○ *Ask people about their feelings.* Most people like it when others are interested in them. So if you ask someone, "How did you feel about what happened?" or "What are you feeling now?" you'll get direct information. Use your emotional imagination to try to guess at other people's feelings and then ask them to see if your instincts about their feelings were accurate.

○ *Show empathy as your skills improve.* You can let people know you really understand them by acknowledging their emotions or sharing your feelings.

- Acknowledge *their* emotions. When Kareem says, "You know, I really don't like the way you looked at me!" you can reply, "I hear that you didn't like my look and you're angry about it." That way Kareem knows you understand both what he said AND how he feels.

- Tell them *you've* been there. You can show that you have some idea of how others are feeling by using the "feel/felt" way of speaking. You can say, "I understand why you feel sad about your dog's death. I felt really sad, too, when my dog was hit by a car." Sharing in this way says that you understand something about what they're going through, that you can relate to them at a feelings level, and that they are not alone with their feelings.

Empathy as a Gift

The ability to empathize brings many gifts. When you communicate using feelings, you connect with people at a more personal level. Empathy strengthens your connections to others, deepens your friendships, and improves your self-understanding.

Empathy improves your ability to understand and care about others. When you're in touch with how others will feel about your actions, you're less likely to be mean or violent in your relationships. When you're in conflict, your ability to empathize will help you take other people's feelings into consideration. Because you understand them better, you'll have a better chance of finding a good solution.

People who can empathize have a richer experience of life. The best way to develop these skills is by practicing in a place where it's okay to express your emotions. This can be with anyone you trust—family, friends, or a group of people who get together for support.

Build a Support Network

Isolation is the biggest danger for people who are having problems in their lives. Typically, the worse people feel, the more they tend to cut themselves off from others. But when we're alone with our fears, worries, and anger, they can easily spiral into huge problems, and our thinking can become twisted in the process.

Can you remember a time when you felt so bad that you said, "Just leave me alone!"? As your isolation grew, you may have felt that you were the only one who had ever experienced what you were going through. You may have felt that no one else could ever understand and that you were the most put-upon, wronged, misunderstood creature that ever walked the face of the planet. While often none of these things are even remotely true, you can get so lost in this kind of negative thinking that you can't find your way to the life-giving support that family members, trusted friends, or a support group can offer.

When we get together with others and openly share our thoughts and feelings, we learn that we're not alone. When you feel safe enough to let people see who you really are, you always discover that others are having or have had similar emotions and that it's possible to find nondestructive ways to deal with even the worst feelings.

Supportive people are very important. Not only will they encourage you to avoid behaviors that are violent and disrespectful to yourself or others, but they will also help you remember how much is right with your life.

Build a support network

114

Someone who is preoccupied with problems tends to forget all the things that are going pretty well. Remembering the upside of your life—the things that are really great (and there are wonderful parts in everyone's life)—keeps you from feeling hopeless and desperate. When you're lost in the hard things, you will need help to see what's right about your life.

What to Look For

When you feel pressurized with uncomfortable feelings, violent thoughts, and increasing isolation, the act of reaching out for support can make the difference between behaving in desperate, misguided ways and finding self-respecting solutions to your problems. The support of trusted individuals or structured groups can be a kind of life preserver. Here are a few things to look for as you set out to build a support network.

> ▶ "I was abused as a
> ▶ young child—physi-
> ▶ cally and mentally.
> ▶ I think the main
> ▶ thing is support. If
> ▶ you can't get it from
> ▶ your home, use your
> ▶ friends, guardians,
> ▶ or any other adult
> ▶ in your life to show
> ▶ you and guide you
> ▶ through life."
> ▶ — Bailey, 16

○ *People you can trust.* Trust is *the* most important thing. If you don't feel totally safe, you won't share the things that trouble you most. We begin to get a sense of how much we can trust people from the first time we meet them. We usually start out revealing the little things to see if they will keep that trust or let us down in some way. If someone is trustworthy, we may take a bigger risk by sharing a little more with him or her. A person who continues to be there for you may eventually become a close friend. Real trust has to be earned over time. When it is present in relationships, people have something very precious.

If you're in a structured support group, trust is really important because you may not know everyone at first. In order to develop trust between members, good support groups have guidelines about how the group operates, including rules about confidentiality and how to handle members who behave in ways that make the group unsafe. In support group settings, you also need a facilitator you feel is trustworthy. Like any other person in the group, the facilitator must earn your trust and be accountable to the group rules.

> ▶ **"I go to my old**
> ▶ **friends for support.**
> ▶ **They know me and**
> ▶ **know when my**
> ▶ **thinking is nuts!"**
>
> — Barty, 18

o *People who will listen.* Really supportive people are great listeners. They let you say what you need to say without judging you, giving you advice, or turning the conversation around to themselves. When you have big problems, you really need to talk, and talk, and talk. Sometimes that's all you need. At other times, you may want to hear another person's perspective. Before offering feedback, a good support person waits until you've asked. Someone who can't just listen or won't make the time to hear you out may still be a friend, but never a best friend.

> ▶ **"The other guys on**
> ▶ **the team are really**
> ▶ **there for me. We**
> ▶ **look out for each**
> ▶ **other and talk**
> ▶ **about our problems**
> ▶ **together."**
>
> — Dwayne, 15

o *People who understand feelings.* We need support when we're lost and confused and at the limits of our ability to cope. That often means we're having strong feelings. In those moments, we need more than just to talk about what's going on; we need to express our feelings. It might mean you'll actually be really sad and cry or show your anger by being really mad. To get great support, you'll want to have connections with people who aren't frightened by feelings, people who can stick with you if you need to be an emotional mess for a while. They won't need to talk you out of your emotions or to "fix" you because you're having feelings.

○ *People who've been there.* You get a special kind of understanding from someone who's had similar problems and challenges. You may want to include people in your support network who have faced challenges similar to yours.

You may want the help of a friend whose parents have divorced, whose brother or sister has died, who's dealing with bullying—or whatever else you may be facing. People who have "been there, done that" will have an easier time understanding what you're feeling and thinking.

They may even have some helpful suggestions about what to do based on their experience. There are special support groups for people who are getting sober, dealing with anger-management issues, or working through a loss. They have proved to be very successful because they bring together people who really understand one another's challenges.

Where to Look for Support

It's best not to wait until you desperately need a support network to try to develop these connections. You can think of your support network as being like a fire extinguisher: you want to know where it is, know how it works, and make sure it's functional long before the fire.

> "My two good friends got mad at me because I wasn't keeping secrets and I was telling everyone everything. They said they couldn't trust me anymore. But we talked about it for a while and I proved to them that I would never betray their trust again."
> — Kelsey, 16

If you don't have a support network when you feel like you're going to burst into flames, look around. There are people at your school, community organizations, places of worship, and crisis centers who will be there for you.

▶ **"I don't really think**
▶ **that I have anyone**
▶ **for support."**
▶
▶ — Justin, 17

While that support is usually very high quality, it's not the same as having a network of familiar and trusted friends to lean on. Trust between people grows over time. If you want to have a functioning support network, you have to find some people who you think would be trustworthy and begin to build your connection to them *before* you're in a crisis.

As you set out to develop a network of support people, a good place to start is right at home. For many kids, parents are the most trustworthy and supportive people in their lives. You may also have trusting relationships with a brother or sister. An aunt, uncle, or grandparent may be easy for you to talk with. You're very lucky if you can trust these people with your feelings about the hard and scary stuff in your life, because you have a great start on a solid network. But lots of young people don't have support from their families. If that's the case for you, there are plenty of other places you can look for people you can count on.

"Both of my parents are easy to talk to and give me advice on everything. I definitely trust my best friend to cry and talk with. She is always there for me and helps me with my problems."

— Kelsey, 16

You may already have connections to supportive people and not realize it. We are attracted to our friends because they are naturally supportive. You may want to look at your circle of friends to see who may have the potential to be a closer friend. If you find someone, you can work at deepening your relationship by gradually sharing more private details about yourself and your life.

If this friend stays true to you, keeps your trust, and remains supportive, you'll have another great addition to your support network.

Besides good friends, many others might be there for you if given the opportunity. For some people, a school counselor, social worker, or private therapist can also be a very reliable source of support. You may have a neighbor, a friend's parent, someone in your spiritual community, or people at school, such as volunteers, teachers, aides, custodians, or security guards, who'd make great connections for you. One or more of these people may be very willing to support you, but until you reach out to

> ▸ **"My mom and sisters**
> ▸ **can always tell if**
> ▸ **something is bother-**
> ▸ **ing me. They would**
> ▸ **take as much time**
> ▸ **as needed to listen**
> ▸ **to me."**
> ▸ — Mary, 16

them, you just won't know. Saying something as simple as, "Would it be okay with you if we spent a little time together? I'd really like to talk to you" might be the beginning of a very important relationship.

You may also want to consider joining a formal support group in your school or somewhere in your community. A formal support group can be great if you want some support in place quickly. This approach to getting help with your problems is a good choice because most people there really want the benefits of the group. The group rules and skills of the facilitator can make them a safe place to share your problems and feelings.

The Gifts in a Support Network

It takes energy to get a support network in place, but the effort is really worth it. Whether you build your own support network or go to an established support group, you'll have a powerful resource for making your life better. It also means you'll always have somewhere to share the hard stuff in your life.

When you have developed a high level of trust with individuals or a support group, your feeling of isolation and the crazy thinking that grows out of being alone with your troubles always decreases. You'll be able to express your feelings, talk about the hard things in your life, and feel validated by others. You'll get to see life through others' eyes and learn from their experiences. In the process, you'll learn how to empathize and develop your feelings vocabulary.

The more you use your supportive relationships, the stronger they get, better equipping you to deal with all your problems. In these relationships, people grow quickly, and the skills you learn will help you the rest of your life.

We all have to live in the world with other people. You have the choice to develop the skills you'll need to make relationships successful or to struggle with anger, conflict, hurt feelings, and confusion—in isolation. Invest in yourself by building a support network.

Chapter 7

What You Can Do at School

So much of what happens to kids at school depends on the position the adults in their schools have taken about violence. A school that draws a hard line against violence in any form has a clear definition of violence and publishes expectations for people's behavior.

Administrators, teachers, counselors, social workers, and other staff, following solid policies and procedures, work together to stop violence. They are trained in how to handle violent behaviors. In those schools, supportive adults listen and take action against violence when they see or hear about it. Students and their families participate in violence prevention, and teachers communicate regularly with parents. This type of school setting is where you'll find the most support for your own violence prevention efforts.

But in just about every school, you will find some adults who are willing to support your efforts, even if the school hasn't taken an official position. So wherever you go to school, you can do something to take a personal stand against violence. Let's look at just a few ways.

Don't Look the Other Way

To do something about violence at school, students and adults have to find the courage to speak out. We all have to break the "no talk" rule and change the thinking that "If it's not happening to me, it's not my problem." We can't just look the other way and pretend we don't see violence. If no one takes a stand, the problem will get worse, and before you know it, violence *will* become your problem.

Take the risk to point out the violence that you see or hear, even in its most innocent-looking forms. (See "The Continuum of Violence," pages 13–15.) When you know it's safe, speak up about violence when you see it happening. If for any reason you're not comfortable taking a direct stand, report what you've seen or heard to an adult you trust—your parents or someone at school, like the principal or assistant principal, guidance counselor,

> "At my school there are a lot of fights. Practically every day you hear of one. I think they're stupid and worthless, and they don't solve anything. I wish I didn't have to deal with it, so I just don't get myself involved."
>
> — Kelsey, 16

social worker, security officer, a teacher, the librarian, or the school nurse. Find someone who will listen and share your concern. Let an adult decide if the problem is serious enough to take action. You wouldn't want to be the person who could have prevented some violent act *if only* you had said something.

> *"It is estimated that 160,000 children miss school every day due to fear of attack or intimidation by other students."*
>
> — National Education Association —

Things You Should Report

If you actually see or hear about someone planning to do anything violent, take it very seriously. If you heard someone talking about committing suicide, you'd certainly take that seriously and get help right away. You need to do the same if you hear about any other possible act of violence. Here is a quick list of things that you *must* report:

○ You hear a person or group threaten to hurt or kill someone.

○ You learn about an individual or group making preparations for a violent act.

○ You see knives, guns, or other weapons.

○ You see someone going through another person's locker, backpack, purse, or clothing.

○ You witness violent behaviors like aggressive pushing, bumping, yelling, tripping, or blocking the way.

○ You hear name-calling, especially when people use racial, religious, or sexual language.

○ You witness the continual harassment of an individual or group.

○ You see people make threatening gestures, including gang signs or symbols.

○ You see someone damage school property or another student's belongings.

We can no longer assume people are "just talking" when they suggest acts of violence. There is too much at risk if someone is serious. Report violence, and remember that the more dangerous the potential for violence, the quicker it should be reported.

"One day another parent called to say she had witnessed my son defending a weaker and less fortunate mainstreamed student whose handicap left him easy prey to the bullies. He had done so by distracting the abusers with humor and dialogue. She was advising me to tell my son he shouldn't get involved because he might get hurt sometime. Without hesitation, I said that I was never more proud of my son . . . and I was afraid I couldn't follow her advice. I said I hadn't raised my son to 'look the other way' and I wasn't going to ask him to change now, because he was on his way to being one great adult."

— A proud mother —

Learn to Deal with Bullying

Bullying is when an individual or group of people deliberately and repeatedly harm or threaten to harm a person or group of people who are less powerful in some way. This behavior is all about the abuse of power—one person picks on someone simply because he or she can. Whether you are the target of bullying or a witness to the ongoing intimidation and humiliation of another student, everyone suffers. This behavior is perhaps the most destructive form of school violence. It's not fair and it can be terrifying.

"Statistics prove that it is highly unlikely that students will be killed in their schools. What's much more likely is that they will be injured emotionally by harassment, bullying, intimidation, discrimination, merciless teasing, and senseless cruelty, all inflicted upon them by their classmates."

— Mary Grace Reed, school board member —

The Bad News about Bullying

Unfortunately, people who bully really enjoy the feeling of power they get from picking on others. This sense of power is different from the real personal strength and self-esteem that comes from being loved, accepted, and having the ability to successfully deal with life's problems.

If you're bullied and you try to fight back, the situation almost always gets worse because the person doing the bullying has to feel more powerful than you and so escalates the level of violence. If you try to be rational and use conflict-management skills, these people will probably laugh you off. They just want to feel powerful, not solve problems. If you cry, show fear, or give in, you'll become an even better target. The bad news about bullying is that it will continue until someone stops it, and to stop bullying, you almost always need adult intervention.

How do

you feel

when you

are a target

of bullying?

▸ *This has to be one of the worst feel-*
▸ *ings in the world. You feel inferior,*
▸ *worthless, and stupid. The only way*
▸ *to react to bullies is to either make*
▸ *a joke of it or let them know that*
▸ *what they are saying REALLY doesn't*
▸ *bother you (even if inside it is killing*
▸ *you). Eventually they will get bored.*
▸ • Daniella, 16

▸ *I always feel horrible, and if I knew a*
▸ *way to stop them, I would.*
▸ • Johnny, 16

▸ *There were people at school who were*
▸ *emotionally violent towards me who I*
▸ *couldn't handle so well. I'm afraid to*
▸ *say I let their bullying get to me so*
▸ *bad, I ended up needing counseling.*
▸ *They were a bunch of really nasty*
▸ *people I'm glad to be rid of.*
▸ • KT, 19

Choosing not to take on a person who is bullying you or others by yourself means that you're smart, not that you're weak or lack courage. Getting an adult involved is the best thing you can do. In some cases, adults don't intervene because they're too busy or don't understand what's happening. But when adults don't intervene, it says that the behavior is acceptable, and the problem gets worse. Usually, if you're willing to ask, you can find a supportive adult. Tell a teacher, counselor, social worker, principal, or assistant principal. If you can't get the attention of someone at school, parents can often help the school administration see how bullying is destructive to the school climate and academic performance of students. If you're being bullied, reach out for adult help, and keep trying until you get it.

"Many students endure torture day upon day that most adults wouldn't tolerate for a moment. This type of intimidation destroys the bond of trust so critical to a healthy school community. Parents and administrators shouldn't pretend bullying doesn't exist just because they don't see the behavior. This form of violence in our schools is routine, invisible, and immensely destructive. If you really want to know if this is a problem in your school, ask the students; they know."

— Mary Grace Reed, school board member —

How to Reduce Bullying

The most obvious way to reduce the amount of bullying in the world is to make sure you're not behaving this way yourself. If you're part of the problem, you can really be making a mess for yourself. When you use power and control over others to get what you want, you make people angry, stir up resentment, and may set yourself up as a target for bullying. In the long run, people who bully always lose. Research indicates that they go on to have a much higher than average chance of being convicted of crimes as adults.

If you tend to bully and are smart enough to see that it's ultimately self-destructive, you can get help. Like so many forms of violence, it has been learned and can be unlearned. To change your behavior, you'll need to ask for support, as well as learn some new skills. The skills described in chapters 5 and 6 are a great place to start. Bullying behavior can be hard to change, but given the long-term costs, your efforts will bring enormous rewards.

▶ **"If you're a bully, violence makes you feel good and the people you're with make you feel good because they suck up to you. But when you get caught, they don't even know you."**

— Lydia, 17

What can

be done

to get kids

to stop

bullying?

Ignoring them is often one of the best ways.

• Rebecca, 16

Tell them to stop, or ask an adult to help.

• Kate, 11

Ignore them. Don't go to their level. It sucks being picked on, but as you get older it gets better.

• Barb, 16

At first, I feel embarrassed. But after a while, I start to feel pity for the bully. They really don't even know me, so nothing they say should have an effect on me. I think in those situations you need to know that "No one can make you feel inferior without your permission."

• Julia, 15

If you are either a target of or a witness to bullying, you can do the following things:

○ **Tell someone.** The instant you witness or become a target of bullying, you need to call attention to it ... and adult attention is best. Bullying often starts with someone doing little things to see if the potential target is vulnerable. If someone doesn't put a stop to the behavior, the person who bullies will keep pushing and may do even more violent things. Standing up to early acts of bullying can stop the problem quickly.

○ **Tell a person who bullies to leave you or others alone.** (See "Develop Assertiveness Skills," pages 95–103.) When you are strong and direct without being aggressive about how you feel, you're much better off than being submissive, showing fear, or behaving like a victim. People who show weakness are magnets for bullying. Assertiveness skills will help, although they may not be enough.

○ **Use any system your school offers for reporting bullying behavior.** If you're uncomfortable talking to someone about being bullied yourself, write down information about the bullying incidents and give this to a trusted adult or turn it in anonymously. When bullying is made public, the behavior often stops.

○ **Try to avoid bullying situations.** Sometimes "out of sight, out of mind" helps. Most bullying occurs in unsupervised areas, like hallways, bathrooms, and locker rooms. You can make sure you're with others when you're in these parts of the school.

○ **Make friends.** People who bully go after individuals who are alone and vulnerable. Making friends is easier said than done if you're shy, but kids who have a group of supportive friends aren't easy targets for bullying. One fast way to build your social circle is to join school clubs and organizations. This will provide a great defense against bullying; plus you'll take part in activities that feed your self-esteem and help you to make connections to others.

"The last of the human freedoms is to choose one's attitude."

— Victor Frankl —
World War II concentration camp survivor
Author of *Man's Search for Meaning*

Practice Acceptance

Many of us feel uncomfortable and want to avoid people we think are different from us. Some people are so intimidated by differences that they form groups made up of "people like us." Without ever bothering to really learn about others, these groups just decide that they are superior to those they see as "not like us." While this is sad enough, some of these people, based on their conclusion of superiority, choose to be violent. The result is that even though we live in a diverse society, each year thousands of people are victimized because of their skin color, ethnicity, religion, gender, sexual orientation, economic status, age, or disability. People who are targets of violent acts of intolerance experience emotional or physical pain that may last for a day or for a lifetime.

> ▶ **"I don't care what**
> ▶ **others say. I'm just**
> ▶ **proud of me and my**
> ▶ **family—not because**
> ▶ **we're Native**
> ▶ **Americans, but**
> ▶ **because we're**
> ▶ **human beings."**
> ▶ — Kristina, 13

It can be all too easy to avoid direct and honest discussions of our differences because they can be confusing, complicated, and sometimes emotionally uncomfortable. For that reason, many people find themselves living in complete ignorance about people who are in some way different from them. But when we don't get to know other people, misconceptions, stereotypes, and fears grow. When that happens, we hold opinions and take actions that are based on our illusions about others, not on reality.

Intolerance of differences can lead us to be violent in a hundred subtle ways. Without even realizing it, our behavior can tell people that they don't count, that they are unacceptable or unlovable. Intolerance can take serious forms, such as name-calling, mocking someone's voice or gestures, telling a demeaning joke, making a threat, or just excluding someone with no explanation. At the very worst, extremely violent acts, like shootings, beatings, and segregation, stem from the unwillingness to accept differences between people.

Being mean to others because they are different is foolish. Current statistics say that high school graduates will change jobs at least seven times over their careers. Because of the increasing diversity in the culture, you'll be working with a huge variety of people as you get older. If you start now to learn to get along with people who are different from you, you'll increase your chances for an interesting, happy, and successful future.

▶ "If you can take the
▶ fear of people who
▶ are different and
▶ deal with it just long
▶ enough to really
▶ hear what the other
▶ person says, under-
▶ stand who they are,
▶ you'll learn a lot and
▶ find out about your
▶ judgments, fears,
▶ and limited point
▶ of view."
▶ — Sally, 46

What is it like to experience discrimination?

I have experienced discrimination because of my race many times, and it's not fun. It was never about me because they never knew me. I always wonder if the person is doing it because they were raised to really believe these things or if they were just trying to impress a bunch of friends by doing something radical.

• Raja, 15

I experienced a great deal of emotional violence at school, not so much physical. I remember when a guy called me a "bloody Jew." It was the first time I had experienced anti-Semitism and it hit me with a big shock. I was furious and terribly hurt.

• KT, 19

Discrimination is really quite degrading and it was really bad for my self-esteem. I was from a different country and had a slightly different accent. I didn't understand why others made such a big deal of the little differences between us, when all it came down to was that we were all human beings anyway. It left me feeling very lost and alone in the world, as well as being so uncertain about every little thing I did. I lost confidence in my own abilities and lost the courage to use my initiative.

• Coyote, 16, New Zealand

The first step toward that future is to accept the fact that people are different. That doesn't mean you have to agree with different points of view or change your life in any way. All that's necessary is to acknowledge that different is simply different, not wrong.

> **"No matter what a person's appearance, you cannot tell what they are like (good or bad) until you get to know their heart."**
>
> — Elizabeth M., 48

People aren't born with hate and prejudice; those attitudes are learned. It's possible to create homes, schools, and communities where prejudice and intolerance are not learned in the first place. And if lessons of violence have already been taught, they can be unlearned. To begin to do that, we all have to understand ourselves better in order to really practice acceptance of others.

"Spend Some Time" Exercise

You may be unaware that subtle intolerance may be influencing your behavior. To get some sense of how your biases may be showing up, spend some time talking with people who are different from you in some way. It's a great way to start to examine your own biases, misperceptions, and judgments.

Spend some time learning to understand a person:

○ who is much younger than you

○ who is much older than you

○ who wears clothes that are very different from those you'd choose

○ whose academic ability and grades are very different from yours

○ whose body type is different from yours

○ who is from another country

○ whose physical capabilities are much more limited than yours

○ who grew up in a very different part of town than you

o whose approach to spirituality is different from yours

o whose race or ethnicity is different from yours

o whose sexual orientation is different from yours

o whose family has a lot more or a lot less
   money than yours

As you read this list, did you feel any
resistance or have little excuses pop into
your head about why you
shouldn't bother?
If you find that you
feel uncomfortable
with any of these
suggestions, it means
you have some work to
do on acceptance. That's
okay, because everyone has biases. The challenge is to learn about
their existence and how they influence our behavior and to learn
that they aren't based on reality.

Once you overcome your fears of differences between yourself
and others, you'll be open to whole new worlds of people. You can
include a wider variety of people in your circle of acquaintances and
learn from their unique experiences. While leaving your comfort zone
takes a little risk, your life will become more interesting. Most important, familiarity reduces fear and radically reduces the chances that
you'll be violent toward someone who is different from you.

Be a Reverse Cliquer

Cliques are exclusive circles of friends who have something in common and screen out people who are different. Clique members find
ways to justify keeping out people they have decided don't meet the
group's standards. In doing so, cliques split the world into "insiders"
and "outsiders." The insiders get the illusion of superiority, but they
cut themselves off from the rest of a rich and interesting world.

Putting people into "us" and "them" camps lays the groundwork for hurt feelings and possible hostilities. Cliques that exclude others based on characteristics over which people have no control, like race, religion, or body type, are practicing a form of discrimination and social violence. Whatever the reason for exclusion, being judged as unworthy to be included leads to mountains of hurt feelings, anger, and sometimes the desire for revenge.

The reverse of a clique is a group with open and flexible membership. Challenge yourself and your friends on your willingness and ability to attract a variety of people into your circle. Or better yet, don't have just one circle of friends. Try having such a wide variety of friends that you're known as someone who gets along with everyone. You'll be amazed at how good it feels to have almost everyone in the hallways going out of their way to say hi to you. Besides reducing social violence, being an inclusive and accepting person makes *you* much more interesting.

▶ **"People who don't make an effort to get along are the only people I have a major bias against. I believe in trying to create and maintain a harmonious environment, but there are always individuals and groups who try and ruin the peace between others."**

— Coyote, 16, New Zealand

▶ **"When I first heard that the Columbine High killers shot people just because their skin was darker or they wore a baseball cap, I was truly surprised. That is unbelievable."**

— Dustin, 13

How do you

feel about

cliques?

> I totally disagree with the whole "clicky" thing, because it causes a lot of problems. People need to accept people for who they are not what they are.
>
> • PAK, 17

> When I was in elementary school, all the kids ignored me. I've heard there's one outsider in every class . . . but it hurt me a lot. It still hurts me. I didn't know why they did it. I still don't know why they did it.
>
> • Joy, 19

> I get sick of the way people act in groups with all that conformity. Non-individuality is what puts you in popular cliques.
>
> • Skip, 17

> I get a lot of crap for being "goth" (I'm NOT—I belong to the Gutter Glitter subculture) and being a lesbian. I've had things thrown at me and been shoved around. I don't respond, but it hurts. It really, really hurts.
>
> • Silverkat, 15

Get Involved

Do you want to really drive a change in how your school deals with violence? You can have a huge impact by getting involved in some of the school groups that have the power to influence policy changes. When people begin to talk about violence, sharing their feelings and experiences in school, things begin to happen. Any way you choose to bring the topic of violence prevention to the attention of your school community can help. Here are a few possibilities:

> "I would love to have the opportunity to start up discussion groups in my school. I would try to get a wide variety of people together to discuss their differences and to act on them in nonviolent ways."
>
> — Maggie, 17

Student Council

The student council can be a forum for organizing groups or activities that can reduce school violence. During the next student council elections, you can work to make school violence prevention a campaign issue. Perhaps you'd be interested in running for a seat on the council to raise awareness, or maybe you'd prefer to work on a friend's campaign. Even if you aren't an elected member of your school's student council, you can encourage student council members to discuss school climate issues or invite you or others to speak at a meeting or school assembly.

Principal's Advisory Committee

Many schools have a principal's advisory committee, which can be composed of students or of a mix of teachers and students. Advisory committees usually meet with the principal monthly to discuss important school issues. In these meetings, the administration gets direct and honest feedback about issues from the students' perspective, and students have the opportunity to influence decisions that impact them. This is a great place to suggest some type of violence awareness or prevention program. If you have an advisory committee in your school, drop your principal a note and ask to be included. If no such committee exists, suggest starting one!

Student-Faculty Forum

At student-faculty forums, students and teachers share their feelings with one another on issues like school climate, student dissatisfaction or problems, or any other hot topic. A neutral person usually facilitates the discussions, so any school issues can be discussed in an honest and open way. This kind of gathering helps students and teachers to better understand the other's view and, in the process, helps develop mutual respect.

A forum is a perfect place to bring up issues of violence, discrimination, or unfair practices. Students usually organize these gatherings. If your school has never had a student-faculty forum and you're really interested, work with your school principal, teacher, counselor, or social worker to start one.

> ▶ **"There are most**
> ▶ **likely others who**
> ▶ ***almost* had the**
> ▶ **nerve to do this but**
> ▶ **didn't. I say don't**
> ▶ **be afraid to take a**
> ▶ **chance; the silence**
> ▶ **of others is not an**
> ▶ **indication of the**
> ▶ **interest level. Start**
> ▶ **small and seek out**
> ▶ **those who will help**
> ▶ **you."**
> ▶ — Michelle, 18,
>   established a
>   student-faculty forum
>   in her senior year

Get People Thinking

Perhaps you're not the type to participate in meetings with a lot of other people. You can create violence prevention awareness in a number of other ways. Here are a few things you can do to get people thinking, talking, and maybe even taking action around the issues of violence.

○ Make posters that use motivational quotes about violence prevention and get permission to put them up in your school.

○ Write an article about the different forms of violence you've seen in your school and submit it to the school or community newspaper.

○ Ask the person who makes morning announcements to include a positive statement about violence prevention.

○ Ask a counselor to form a support group for people who've been perpetrators or targets of bullying.

○ Encourage the drama instructor to do a short play about violence.

○ Encourage your school to offer parenting classes. Many parents are without parenting skills—huge numbers of kids grow up in family settings that set them up for violent behavior. Most students will be parents someday, so it makes sense that a critical skill like how to raise great kids should be taught at school.

> "My freshman year at a pep rally, the cheerleaders did a
> game to see who could scream, yell, and demolish the
> national anthem the best. I'm patriotic and didn't like
> it, so I wrote to the school paper expressing my feelings.
> I got a violent response from others as a result, but I
> refused to respond to violence with violence. I just fought
> them with my freedom of speech and the press."
> — Maggie, 17

Become a Peer Mediator

Programs aimed at teaching people how to prevent or work through conflict are an important component in breaking the circle of violence at school. The National Association for Mediation in Education reports that in schools employing mediation and conflict-management programs, students show decreased numbers of detentions and suspensions, less victimization, increased self-esteem, a greater sense of personal control, and higher academic performance. All of these factors can make a big difference in reducing violence in your school.

In peer mediation programs, selected students get special training in conflict-management and negotiation skills. These students then become a resource for others who have conflicts that they can't solve by themselves. Students who are stuck in their differences and are getting increasingly frustrated with each other can benefit from the objectivity a young person outside the problem can offer.

A successful peer mediation session follows a process:

1. The peer mediator helps the people involved agree on the ground rules; for example, promising to be honest and respectful, to keep the discussion confidential, to refrain from physical violence and name-calling, and to listen quietly when someone else is speaking.

2. The peer mediator asks each person for his or her version of what happened. Each person gets to say both what happened and how he or she feels as a result. All participants should reach a clear understanding about what happened and the feelings involved.

> "I was in a fight in seventh grade. I was getting tired of another student who would tease me about everything I did. We finally fought and it didn't solve a thing. What really helped was a mediation the two of us had where we talked about why things were the way they were."
>
> — Brian, 16

3. The participants look for solutions. Each person talks about what he or she could have done differently. Each person also gets a chance to talk about what he or she needs for the conflict to end.

4. After exploring possible solutions, the students agree to a set of outcomes that are comfortable for each of them. Sometimes people even write up and sign their agreements to show they are committed to carrying them out. The session ends by acknowledging the end of the conflict in some way.

In addition to the satisfaction of helping people find nonviolent solutions to their issues, peer mediators get excellent training in relationship skills that will help them throughout life. Get involved by becoming a peer mediator. If your school doesn't have a peer mediation program, ask about starting one. Collect information on programs from other schools or the Internet, and then see if you can get a teacher, social worker, or counselor to support the idea.

> ▶ **"I like to hear what**
> ▶ **others say. And if I**
> ▶ **can listen to them,**
> ▶ **they can listen to**
> ▶ **me. I give them**
> ▶ **respect and basic-**
> ▶ **ally expect it back."**
> ▶ — ALJ, 17

Find a School Advocate

An advocate is someone you can count on for support. You'll want an adult from your school on your side when you decide to do something about violence. An adult advocate can be invaluable for personal support and can help you meet the challenges of launching an idea or a new program at your school.

If you can get support from the school administration, you may be able to make a big difference in the school climate. The principal or other administrators may welcome your interest and be willing to support you in your violence prevention efforts. But sometimes students are not comfortable even being seen in the administrative offices where these school staff work. So they need other options.

School counselors can be a great source of personal support as well as a source of ideas for how you might change the school climate. School social workers, whose offices typically aren't in the administrative area, are another excellent alternative to the administration for helping you with your efforts. They'll respond to reports of potential violence or incidents of bullying and can work with you on activities to reduce violence. Because of their training, both social workers and counselors are ideal partners. These professionals care about young people and may have a strong interest in and good advice about any ideas you have that can reduce violence.

Even by taking what may seem like minor actions, you can make a difference in your school. A series of small acts has a way of adding up to new awareness and changed behaviors. Your efforts will touch more lives than you'll ever imagine, and you'll feel better about yourself for doing something about a huge problem. As your skills and motivation grow, you may even want to expand your efforts. Believe it or not, you can also reduce violence in your neighborhood, your community, and the world.

What You Can Do in Your Community and the World

CHAPTER 8

As you get further away from the parts of your life that you can influence directly, it may seem harder and harder to make the BIG changes. But you can have a major impact on the violence in the community where you live and in the big world out there.

By working on your own and joining with others, you can create a more peaceful world. Here is a short list of suggestions to start your thinking.

Be a Mentor

Young people who have the help, guidance, and unconditional support of an older mentor can overcome incredible obstacles on the way to becoming successful people. Research shows that young people who have mentors are more apt to succeed at school, grow self-esteem, learn critical relationship skills, and be optimistic about their futures.

Everyone needs mentoring. We all need people we can look up to as role models. A mentor offers a unique type of positive attention. Think how good it would feel to have someone who shows interest in your life, cares about how you're doing, gives you information that helps you in life, and regularly tells you that you're an incredible person. When people have that kind of supportive relationship, they're less likely to feel alone with their problems, fill up with angry feelings, and lash out with violence.

While it's important for young people to have adult mentors, we can all be mentors, regardless of our age. You can make a huge difference in the life of a younger person just by being yourself and offering positive attention. You don't have to join a formal mentor program or get special training. Just informally adopt someone younger than you in your neighborhood or school. Spend a little time and show genuine interest in what's going on in his or her life. Tell this young person what positive qualities you see in him or her. It's not hard to do. Even a few minutes of concentrated positive attention on a regular basis can make a huge difference in a person's life. If you want to take your mentoring even more seriously, volunteer at an after-school program, church youth group, or programs run by the local park board or other community agencies. There are younger kids everywhere, and any one of them would benefit from a regular and positive relationship with you.

Mentoring is never a one-way street. In addition to what you'll learn from another person (yes, even a "kid" younger than you!), you get enormous rewards from seeing someone thrive on your compliments and encouragement. It's satisfying to see someone make healthy changes in his or her life because of a relationship with you. You may fill in a critical blank in this younger person's life that will enable him or her to avoid a disaster down the road. Mentoring makes a difference in the world, one life at a time.

Care about Your Community

In communities where people know each other, care about what happens in their neighborhoods, and have a sense of community pride, violence has a more difficult time getting a foothold. You can help by getting involved in programs that build your community's resistance to crime and violence. Here are just a few to consider.

Take a Night Out

The annual National Night Out is observed across the nation one evening in the first week of August. This program is designed to heighten awareness about crime and violence prevention, generate local support for anticrime programs, and foster neighborhood spirit. Communities celebrate in a wide variety of ways. Neighborhoods may organize block parties, parades, visits from police officers, and anticrime and antidrug rallies. Sometimes they host ice-cream socials, cookouts, contests for children, or sporting matches. Whatever they choose to do, the important thing is that people visibly come out to say no to crime and violence and to claim the right to live in peace. By building partnerships between people in the neighborhood and between the neighborhood and the police, events like National Night Out go a long way in helping to reduce crime.

If you haven't heard anything about the event in your neighborhood, call your chamber of commerce or visit the National Night Out Web site at *www.nno.org*. You can find out what other neighborhoods and communities are doing and check the directory of participating communities. With a little assertiveness, effort, and help from others, you might start the program in your neighborhood. Talk to people, hand out information, and see what you can organize. Getting even a few homes to stand up against crime and violence is a great contribution to the safety of your community.

Watch Out for the Neighborhood

Neighborhood Watch is a crime and violence prevention program in which neighbors cooperate with each other and law enforcement to build a safer community. Neighbors become familiar with each others' families, habits, and vehicles. They know when something out of the ordinary is going on and call 911 to report suspicious activity. You can prevent a crime by being willing to make that call.

As part of the program, the police come to a neighborhood gathering and teach home safety and crime prevention tips. When you and you neighbors participate in Neighborhood Watch, you provide extra eyes to help the police. Neighborhood Watch does NOT mean you confront crime suspects or take any personal risks. It's simply neighbors looking out for neighbors and caring about the community.

If your neighborhood decides to have a formal Neighborhood Watch program, you can attend meetings, read the materials, make phone calls, and volunteer to make copies or deliver information around the neighborhood. But even if there's not a formal watch program where you live, you can get involved in neighborhood violence prevention in other ways:

o *Know your neighbors.* Take the time to introduce yourself and explain to them how knowing each other better can reduce crime.

o *Be observant and always report any crimes or suspicious behavior to 911.* The police would much rather come out before a crime or violent act has occurred.

o *Be knowledgeable about crime prevention measures.* Ask your local police about personal safety actions that you can take, or ask if there is a neighborhood watch program near you. Another option is to put "Neighborhood Watch" into an Internet search engine and discover what people in communities all across the country are doing to make their neighborhoods safe.

By being part of a Neighborhood Watch program, you'll feel a sense of pride and accomplishment for doing something important to reduce crime and violence in your community. In addition, you just might make a few new friends who live close by.

Clean, Paint, and Plant

The physical condition of a neighborhood is a statement of ownership and caring. If neighbors work to improve areas that attract undesirable activities, the people committing these acts will get the message to move out. If any part of your city, community, or neighborhood is failing, everyone is in trouble. That's why we all need to help however we can.

Community improvement projects are a great way to get involved. Some neighborhoods set aside special days for paint-a-thons, trash cleanup, graffiti removal, planting trees and flowers, and many other types of events. One benefit of these projects is that various people come together with the common goal of community improvement. When you participate, you'll feel the determination and power of people organized to do something constructive about crime and violence.

But you don't have to wait for an official event to come along. Do what you can do in front of your own house or on your own street. Organize a few friends to pick up trash on the street or in empty lots. Plant a few flowers in a visible place. Help out a sick or elderly person in your neighborhood who can't handle home or yard maintenance. There are plenty of small things you can do to make a BIG statement that others will notice. You'll feel the pride that comes from taking action to prevent violence by caring about your community.

Support Gun Safety

Some studies show that having guns in a community increases the potential for violence. Yet many people keep handguns in their homes for protection. Those guns kill more family members than intruders. The American Academy of Pediatrics reports that 8 percent of children accidentally injured or killed with guns are shot in their own home or the home of relatives or friends. It's clear that a lot of hurt and pain can be avoided by practicing gun safety. If someone in your home has a gun, ask him or her to take the following precautions to minimize the possibility of the gun being misused:

○ Keep guns locked up.

○ Store bullets separately from the gun.

○ Don't hide guns under pillows or next to the bed.

▶ **"Violence with guns has killed a lot of teenagers my age. I sometimes wish it was all just a big bad dream, but it's reality."**

— Gilda, 16

○ Make sure children know that guns are not playthings and are not to be touched under any circumstances.

○ Child-proof guns with trigger locks.

○ Take gun-safety lessons.

You can make a handout with these gun-safety suggestions and distribute it in your neighborhood. That act alone could save a life.

Get MADD

Mothers Against Drunk Driving (MADD) is not just a bunch of moms angry about drinking. It's a nationwide organization made up of thousands of people, including teens, who have joined together to stop drunk driving and to support victims of this violent crime. According to MADD, each day eight young people die in alcohol-related crashes. If you want to help stop a major killer of young people, join forces with these motivated individuals. In addition to the issue of drinking and driving, MADD is working to make communities safer by supporting seat belt use, bicycle helmet use, restrictions on alcohol advertising, and zero tolerance for underage alcohol use.

This organization is especially interested in new ways to reach young people with its message. You can become involved in a local chapter of MADD or at the state or the national level. Another way you can carry MADD's message to others is through your personal behavior. Be a role model to those you know—don't drink, and encourage other teens to make the same choice.

"You must be the change you wish to see in the world."

— Mahatma Gandhi —

Vote against Violence

When you vote, you consider all the alternatives and then take a stand for what you believe in. The great thing about voting against violence is that you don't have to wait for an official election or for others to put the issue on the ballot. Whenever you encounter violence during your day, you can choose to vote against it.

Taking a stand against violence takes commitment, courage, and willingness to take a little pressure from people who are comfortable with violence in their lives. But unless people take a firm and visible stand against violence, it will continue to increase.

What follows are just a few ways you can vote against violence.

Vote with Your Attention

How we spend our time and attention is one way we vote. To vote with your attention means you'll reconsider how much of your time you'll give to some of the sources of violent messages around you. While you have to decide your degree of commitment, consider not giving your attention to:

▶ **"I will refuse to be**
▶ **a part of violence.**
▶ **I will not be a**
▶ **bystander, but**
▶ **instead stand up**
▶ **for what I know is**
▶ **right, peacefully."**
▶ — Kari, 16

○ *Television.* Are you willing to avoid TV programs with unnecessarily violent content? This includes shows or movies about police and criminals shooting it out, gang violence, and science fiction programs that show violence between aliens and humans or in other worlds. This commitment also includes walking away or changing the station on many sporting events, comedy shows, and even some cartoons.

> *"If there's violence and sex [on your TV],*
> *it's because you turn it on."*
>
> — Bill Cosby —

○ *Music.* Will you commit not to listen to music that suggests violence of any kind?

○ *Movies.* Will you take a personal stand and not watch violent movies at the theater or on video?

○ *Computer games.* Will you make a commitment not to play any computer game that involves violence?

These actions may sound drastic, but it's a small part of what's involved if you're really going to vote against violence. Try to make violence-free entertainment choices for a week or a month and see how you feel. You may just discover you feel better when you don't have all that violence flooding in, and it's likely you'll get a bump in self-esteem because you're actually doing something against violence in the world. Without realizing it, you may be inspiring others to take a stand too.

Vote with Your Dollars

The Constitution guarantees the right to free speech, which means the media and manufacturers have the right to produce violent programs and products, but you have the right to refuse to buy them. You can vote with your dollars by making a commitment not to spend your money (or asking a parent not to spend his or her money) on music, movies, computer games, or sporting events that contain violence. In many cases, commercials or print ads also support violent forms of entertainment. You can go the extra mile and not purchase products advertised during programs or events that contain violence.

When lots of people quit supporting violence with their dollars, people that sell violence begin to get the message. Dollars have a lot of clout, so use your economic power.

> "I went to a movie starring Sylvester Stallone. I was shocked at the violence. It never seemed to end. . . . [Stallone] would bash someone's face in, and then shoot up his knees, then kick him, knock him to the ground . . . then continue kicking him in the back, stomach, groin, smashing his face/head into the ground. . . . It went on and on and on. It was horrible. Do people truly need this kind of behavior as entertainment? I have never seen a movie like that before in my life, and will never go to another Stallone movie again because of it."
>
> — Ruth, 38

Vote with Your Pen

If you REALLY want to make a powerful difference with your vote against violence, you can write letters or e-mail. Votes cast with your attention and with your dollars, while power-ful, are pretty anonymous. But when you write to the companies whose movies, toys, computer games, music, television programming, and videos you'll no longer be purchas-ing or viewing and tell them *why* you're boycotting them, you get their attention.

Express your opinions to tele-vision and radio stations, network execu-tives, and advertisers. Tell them what you don't like and what you'd like to see in place of the violence. Ask them to use the power of their medium to do something to reduce violence in the world. You can find addresses for products on the packaging and addresses for tele-vision networks and local stations in *TV Guide*. In "Web Resources" at the back of this book (see pages 165–168), you'll find Internet addresses for sites like the National Coalition on Television Violence and the Center for Media Literacy. On sites like these, you can find sample letters and addresses for movie studios, television networks, and video game manufacturers.

You can also express your opinion about violence in your school or city newspaper. Write to your state legislators and your governor. While you're at it, you can also write to your federal legislators and even the president. For the cost of a stamp (or for free if you use e-mail), you can be one of the growing numbers of voices that are taking a loud and clear stand against violence. (To find your repre-sentatives, check the Vote Smart Web site: *www.vote-smart.org*.)

Why not go a step farther and publicize your violence prevention goals by creating a Web page? You can post local happenings and information on violence prevention programs in your school and community.

If each one of the many thousands of readers of this book were to send just one letter to vote against violence, the impact would create a substantial buzz. If everyone who reads this book were to get a bunch of friends together to organize a letter-writing campaign, the antiviolence message would grow to a roar!

Vote with Your Feet

Another way you can vote is to take a literal and visible stand against violence in your community. You can participate in rallies against gangs, violence in the media, alcohol-related accidents, guns in the community, or illegal drugs. Sometimes, in reaction to a violent incident, people gather to demonstrate against violence as a way to heal from the loss. When people stand together to show the world how they feel about the destructive forces of violence, they send a powerful message. And your presence will add one more solid vote.

Vote with Your Mouth

Possibly the most powerful vote you can cast is the easiest to do. Every time you witness an act of violence and it's safe for you to speak up, say something about how you feel. Say something each time you hear a disrespectful comment, see someone damaging property, witness sexual harassment, see someone being put down or teased, notice an aggressive gesture, or witness someone being pushed, tripped, or hit.

Don't pretend that it's not your problem or that you don't care about what happened. Find the courage to speak up and be counted as someone against violence in any form. Report violent behaviors to adults you trust who can do something if you don't feel safe speaking up yourself.

Millions of people say they are against violence. But until each of us takes action, the influence of violence in our lives will grow. It is up to you. Vote!

▶ **"To reduce violence**
▶ **in the world, be a**
▶ **lighthouse. By**
▶ **giving an example**
▶ **of what is right**
▶ **(being nonviolent),**
▶ **you can have a**
▶ **major impact on**
▶ **others."**
▶ — Jeremy, 16

Use Internet Connections

The Internet has become a powerful resource for people who want to take action against violence. With this incredible tool, you can connect with, support, influence, and learn from people all over the world. You'll gain access to an incredible array of information, organizations, and individuals. Here are just a couple of ways you can use the Internet.

All Internet browsers have a search capability. You can click on the search button and enter words such as *violence prevention, school violence, community violence, family violence, bullying, violence in the media* . . . just about any form of violence you can imagine. You'll be taken to a list of literally hundreds of Web sites on these subjects. Each one of these sites will list great information, suggested activities, and people to contact. In addition, most Web sites have links to other Web sites on the subject. Don't forget to visit the Web site for this book at **www.thehumanvolcano.com**. It contains current links and access to important resources, as well as gives you the opportunity to read more comments about violence from teens and to contribute your thoughts.

E-mail is a powerful, instant, global, and free way to connect with others. You can e-mail your friends and the people in your school and community who may be working on violence prevention projects. You may even find your e-mail address book growing to include people from all over the country and the world.

You can participate in on-line discussions with others who are interested in doing things to reduce violence in the world. The Internet offers on-line communities for people who share common interests. In these virtual communities, you can join chat rooms and trade ideas, information, and encouragement with your on-line friends—no matter where they live. The Internet is an important tool for reducing violence wherever in the world you may live.

"The world is too dangerous to live in—not because of the people who do evil, but because of the people who sit and let it happen."

— Albert Einstein —

Risk Action

You can do many things to reduce violence in your relationships, school, and community. But to make anything happen, you'll have to DO something, and that means taking risks:

○ *You'll have to risk behaving in new ways with your friends.* They may like your old behaviors and not be comfortable with your new stand against violence. Some friends may not want to go along with your choices and may even move away from you because of your position. Standing up to violence is not always socially comfortable.

○ *You'll have to take a visible stand against violence.* While you'll probably get a lot of support, some people may not agree with your position. You certainly don't want to do anything to put yourself in danger, but doing something about violence means defending your beliefs and actions.

○ *You may need to work closely with adults to get something started in your school or community.* This can be difficult and uncomfortable at first if you're not used to having a working relationship with adults. But it's great training for life after graduation, and you may even find some new adult friends.

○ *You'll have to risk the possibility that you won't accomplish all of your initial goals.* It's not easy to start something new and to get people interested and willing to donate their time. But even if you don't have a huge success, you'll have taken a stand and become a role model for others. You'll have improved your own knowledge about violence and increased others' awareness of the issues. Most important, you'll be smarter and more experienced the next time you develop a plan.

You'll take some risks when you stand up for what you think is important and try to make a difference. But if no one takes those risks, if no one does anything, things will *not* stay the same. Violence that is not addressed always gets worse. The world desperately needs people not just to say no to violence, but to DO something about it. Start small, keep it simple, and let it grow.

Having Hope

The huge challenge of reducing violence in the world can seem overwhelming, and it's very easy to slip into hopelessness. The problem is so big and so scary, it's just easier to pretend things aren't that bad, hope that someone else will take a stand, and not do anything at all. But when people don't act, life will get worse for all of us.

Just as it takes a combination of forces to produce violence, a group of people acting together can also prevent violence. In addition to doing the things you can do by yourself, you can join others facing this challenge. Right now in your school, neighborhood, or community, you'll find people working to reduce the problem of violence, and they can use your help.

Throughout the history of the United States, groups of motivated people have made impressive changes. Slavery was abolished, women won the right to vote, and the tobacco industry was made to pay for its crimes. In the same way, people are coming together to do something about the problem of violence in our lives. You can join them; you can play a role; you can be part of the growing crowd of people doing something to stop violence.

Hope is about possibilities, and lots of people with hope who are willing to act can make a huge difference. It's your future, so keep the faith, work with others, and do what you can do. Together we will make a difference.

▶ **"You tell young people**
▶ **to stop It [violence]**
▶ **because we are the**
▶ **future and If we**
▶ **don't straighten up**
▶ **our future Is gonna**
▶ **be worse."**

— Jacob, 18,
  Red Wing
  correctional facility

▶ **"Try not to be a violent person. It only hurts yourself and**
▶ **those that care about you . . . and believe me, people**
▶ **who care about you do exist. There Is so much more to**
▶ **life than anger and hurt, so let's all work for that and let**
▶ **go of the pain."**
▶ — Willie, 15

 # CHAPTER 10

What Kids Have Learned about Violence

We asked young people what they'd want to say to those of you reading this book. Some of their comments follow.

"If you know you're violent and out of control, look into getting some help, and talk to someone about it before you do something stupid."
> • Sarita, 16

"Violence is not worth it, it gets you nowhere, and it doesn't make you look cool."
> • Alejundro, 16

"Anger is like chips of ice in my bloodstream.
Anger is like a parasite eating away at me.
Anger is danger without the D."
> • Dwayne B., 21,
>   New York correctional facility, incarcerated since the age of 16

"Violence isn't cool. You should learn to talk things out instead of fighting. Be the bigger person and walk away."
> • BM, 17

"Fighting is an uneducated way to try and solve problems. An educated person knows enough to walk away and leave the other person looking stupid."
> • Kelly, 16

"Violence is not the way.
It just pushes you away
From the pain."
> • Heather, 16

"Tell parents that if they want a violence-free world, they should start with themselves and make sure they are involved in their kid's life."
> • Meaghan, 14

"I would say that violence isn't worth it, it's a waste of time, and there's no point in doing violence to yourself or others. It's better just to get along."
> • Matt, 13

"I would say, no matter what anyone says, even your parents, all the choices you make in life are yours and can only be left up to you. So take responsibility and do what you think is right."
  • Brian, 16

"Treat others as you would like to be treated. Live as God wants you to live. Life is too short to be angry all of the time—put your pride aside and apologize."
  • Kelsey, 16

"Violence, wildness, what's the point?
Lose an arm or a leg or whatever joint.
It makes no sense so try not to be tense.
Stay loose and choose the right thing."
  • Francois, 16

"Promoting understanding between people is the best way to stop violence. People insult each other verbally and assault one another on the mental level because they don't know someone, don't understand them, or don't like them because they are different. If people would just accept differences from person to person and understand that everyone is their own person with different views and opinions and accept others' rights, there would be less conflict."
  • Justin, 17

"If I could say one thing to any young person, it would be not to care what others think. Love yourself first; it's the only way!"
  • Daniella, 16

"Try to think before you act. Do you want to be locked up? If you've got a caring mom, do you want her to cry when she sees you in a coffin? You may not think it can happen—well, it can."
  • Mijamia, 17,
    Red Wing correctional facility

"You deal with wanting revenge in a good way by talking to someone for help. You deal with it in a bad way by doing ANYTHING to get back at the person you're after."

    • Melvin, 18,
      Red Wing correctional facility

"I think the best idea is to accept that there have always been and will always be differences. Billions of people have dealt with it kindly and without violence. It would be nice if everyone just tried it."

    • Aedra, 16

"I'd say that violence really doesn't get you anywhere. If you have problems with someone, just talk about it and maybe get a third person to help you out."

    • Peter, 17

Web Resources

There are too many great Web sites about violence prevention to list here, so we went ahead and created a site of our own:

http://www.thehumanvolcano.com/

By going to this site, you'll find links to the Web sites listed below and many more. When you visit these sites, you'll find ideas for action, up-to-date research data, lists of good books on every aspect of violence, and information about how to contact others who want to reduce violence in the world.

Because of the changing nature of the World Wide Web, we can only guarantee that the information on the sites we've included below was current at the time of publication. Current listings will be maintained at the Human Volcano Web site.

Center for Media Literacy: *http://www.medialit.org/*
The Center for Media Literacy develops and distributes educational materials and programs that promote critical thinking about the influence media has on our lives—from television to T-shirts, from billboards to the Internet. On the "Articles" page, you'll find information on how to start a postcard campaign.

Columbine Healing Web Site: *http://www.columbinehealing.org/*
This Christian Web site contains both stories from and messages to the students at Columbine High School.

Connect for Kids: *http://www.connectforkids.org/*
Anyone can work to make the lives of kids safe, and everyone has a stake in doing so. Connect for Kids offers tips on what you can do in your home, school, and community. Good stuff for adults and kids.

Lion and the Lamb Project: *http://www.lionlamb.org/*
This group sponsors Violent Toy Trade-Ins throughout the country.
To express their desire for a more peaceful world, children bring in
violent toys and transform them into a peace sculpture. They also
sponsor Peaceable Play Days and nonviolent toy sales.

Make the Peace:
http://www.angelfire.com/mn/makethepeace/index.html
This site describes one community's effort at peacemaking. The site
contains a nonviolence pledge and information about a citizen youth
council as well as their Understanding Nationalities in Today's Youth
program (UNITY).

Mike's Movie Violence Count:
http://magi.com/~rhdf/scms/scms.html
This is a really cool page on movie violence. It lists the total number of
simulated murders movie stars have committed throughout their film
career and lists, by movie, how many murders are depicted. This page
keeps track of information on movies that date back to the early 1980s.

Mothers Against Drunk Driving (MADD):
http//www.madd.org/under21/default.shtml
This is MADD's under-21 section, which contains lots of great facts
and information about youth programs. There's a student activist
section, a calendar of events, and a way to search for the MADD
chapter in your state.

National Institute on Media and the Family:
http://www.mediafamily.org/
The National Institute on Media and the Family conducts research
and provides information and education about the impact of the
media on kids and families. When you go to this Web site, check
out ScoreCard, where you'll find MediaMeasure, an interactive quiz
to evaluate your family's media habits. Another cool page, KidScore,

reviews the content of television shows, movies, and video/computer games for violence, illegal behavior, fear, and language.

National School Safety Center: *http://www.nssc1.org/*
The National School Safety Center was created in 1984 to provide additional training and preparation in the area of school crime and violence prevention. The site has information on Safe Schools Week and School Safety Studies.

Neighborhood Watch: *http://washington.xtn.net/~jcpb/neigh.htm*
This page is just one of the many thousands of responses to a search on "Neighborhood Watch." This particular site from Johnson City, Tennessee, contains information on how to protect your home, your neighborhood, yourself, and your car; how to spot a con artist; and how to report suspicious activities. Although this page is for a specific city, it and others like it can provide lots of tips on how to start a Neighborhood Watch program wherever you live.

Teachers for Resisting Unhealthy Children's Entertainment:
http://www.nctvv.org/nctv%20images/action.htm
This Web address takes you right to the organization's "Action" page, which lists the addresses of the major TV networks, toy manufacturers, and government agencies. It even provides sample letters for people who are willing to write letters to speak up against violence.

Teens, Crime, and the Community: *http://www.nationaltcc.org/*
Teens, Crime, and the Community (TCC) is a nationwide effort implemented at the local level to reduce the incidence of teen violence and to engage teens as crime prevention resources in their schools and communities. With their help you might set up a TCC program in your neighborhood.

Violence Prevention Resources: *http://www.child.net/violence.htm*
Violence Prevention Resources is one of several new, comprehensive
resource guides for children and youth. The resources on this page
can help you, your school, neighborhood, or city to learn what fosters
violence and what can be done to keep kids safe. Lots of good statistics and "to do" suggestions.

Youth as Resources: *http://www.yar.org/*
Youth as Resources (YAR) is a community-based program that provides small grants to young people to design and carry out service
projects that address social problems and contribute to significant
community change. The site lists great ideas for community projects
and even the possibility of getting funding for your violence prevention project!

Index

A

acceptance, 133–34, 135

addiction, 66–67

advertising, 41, 152, 153

aggressive behavior, 38, 44, 97, 99
    parental acceptance of, 23–25
    in schools, 25–26
    and self-injury, 67

alcohol, 66–67, 149–50

anger, 44, 85, 88, 90
    accepting responsibility for, 93
    benefits of, 94
    cooling down, 87
    expression of, 43, 86, 88, 94
    feelings behind, 46–47, 86
    holding in, 86, 104
    indirect, 99–100
    physical reactions to, 90–93
    responses to, 6, 88–89, 93–94
    retaliation for, 83, 84

anger management skills, 25, 89–95, 106

assertiveness, 95–97, 129
    benefits of, 102–3
    skills for, 25, 100–102, 107

B

biases, 133–34

body language, 112

boxing, 42

bullying, 26, 98, 125–29
    needs adult intervention, 125–26, 128, 129
    reducing, 127–29

C

canaries, 5, 46–47

cartoons, 35–36, 151

chat rooms, 156

circle of violence, 19, 82–85, 104

cliques, 26, 134–36

commercials. *See* advertising

communities
    improvement projects in, 147–48
    violence in, 29–31
    violence prevention in, 145–48, 149–50

computer games, 22, 38–39, 40, 151, 152
    boycotting, 153

Respect & Protect

This curriculum will help school administrators, teachers, and staff, as well as community members, to recognize and diffuse potential behavior problems before they escalate into violence. *Respect & Protect* will help your school and community to develop a violence prevention and intervention policy. Complete set includes video, manual, 25 *Solving Violence Problems in Your School* booklets, and 25 *Violence in School* booklets.
Order no. 3038

Other books by Earl Hipp:

Feed Your Head: Some Excellent Stuff on Being Yourself

This book of cartoons, essays, and quotes from teens really appeals to students. Topics range from anger, body image, and personal goals to why people use drugs.
Order no. 5034

Help for the Hard Times: Getting through Loss

Earl Hipp addresses loss from the perspective of the heart. He discusses young people's experiences with grief and helps them figure out ways to continue functioning after loss. This book will provide teens with tools to grieve and ways to keep their losses from becoming overwhelming.
Order no. 1332

The Caring Circle

The complete advisor-advisee curriculum will help to develop broad-based support groups for teens who are age twelve or older.
Order no. 0847

For price and order information or a free catalog, please call our telephone representatives or visit our Web site.

▧ HAZELDEN°

1-800-328-9000 (Toll free U.S. and Canada)
1-651-213-4000 (Outside the U.S. and Canada)
1-652-213-4590 (24-Hour Fax)
www.hazelden.org

15251 Pleasant Valley Road
P.O. Box 176
Center City, Minnesota 55012-0176